Black Grief
and
Soul Therapy

DR. NICHOLAS C. COOPER-LEWTER

Richmond
Harriet Tubman Press

Copyright ©1999 by Nicholas C. Cooper-Lewter

All rights reserved. No part of the book may be used or reproduced in any manner whatsoever without prior written permission of the publisher.

Published by Harriet Tubman Press

Library of Congress
Cataloging-in-Publication Data

Cooper-Lewter, Nicholas C.
Black Grief and Soul Therapy
Library of Congress Catalog Card Number 99-71529
ISBN: 1-893652-00-X

Printed in the United States of America

Fourth Printing
August 2003

To All Soul Therapists
Past, Present, and Future

~ *Contents* ~

Foreword

1	Introduction	1
2	Black Grief	17
3	Spiritual Abuse	47
4	Soul Therapy	79
5	Conclusion	115

Postscript 129

Bibliography 135

Index 146

~ *Foreword* ~

As a consultant I have often gone into situations at the request of people who have said to me, "Come in, we're having problems; let us know what we need to do." However, once I help them articulate their problems, they get angry and want to send me home. In such instances, I think, I was not having their problems at home! So I could not have been the source of their problems! But sending me away, I suppose, solves whatever was wrong.

I see this same reaction all the time in counseling. One person begins to get better, and then a spouse or parent says to me, "You've destroyed my marriage," or "You've caused my son or daughter to disrespect me." So now I warn people: if you really want this person to heal, you need to participate in the healing; if only one of you starts to get free, the other is going to be upset, angry, and vulnerable.

In other words, I know from experience what risk I am taking in writing and presenting this book: discomfort often accompanies certain kinds of discovery. In general the degree of this discomfort correlates directly

Trials of being a healer

Risks of initiating challenge and change

FOREWORD

to the amount of energy that has been invested in a certain world view, belief, or configuration of power and privilege. If people have put a great deal of energy into holding things the way they have been, and have done so for a long time, then much energy is needed to move what has been stable; and often the mover or healer bears the brunt of people's anger when they are made to confront challenge and change.

We who are soul therapists will always be tempted to dilute the bitter cup of challenge and change so that it is palatable to the community we love, but we can be encouraged in that an indigenous tradition is coming down to us from the most courageous of our early forebears: soul therapists who did not simply cope with the immensity of the grief among their people but who helped the community to process and overcome the grief.

Indigenous tradition of soul therapy

My friends tell me that whenever they call I am as consistent in answering the phone with "May I help you?" as I am in signing off with "Thank you." So with regard to any candor the reader may detect as I offer my help, and particularly as I confront the Legion of devils in our culture, please understand that when I sit down before a piece of paper to write, I am sitting with something inanimate that cannot love. My friends tell me that I am at my best when interacting with and within community as a teacher, speaker, workshop leader, and counselor—as a soul therapist.

To those friends and loved ones who encouraged me to write this book, I express my deepest gratitude: especially to Leon, who had to die to demonstrate the destructive power of black grief; Stephanie, who has inspired me to live beyond my own grief by forgiving me of my imperfections; and Courtney, who has shown me time and time again why the future holds hope. To those colleagues whose comments have been helpful in the writing of this book, I am also grateful: Alton B. Pollard III, Belva Brown Jordan, Donna Champ Banks, Ghazala Hashmi, and Jon Michael Spencer.

Thank you.

1

~ *Introduction* ~

"Here we have some bodies," the Creator says. "Pick a female or male model and the fitting extremities. The parts are made to fit together, don't worry. Now, pick a color."

Stuffing our DNA into a sperm and egg, God has each of us wait for some fitting get-together in the appropriate part of town and bedroom. As we wait, we ponder the question of what exactly we might have gotten ourselves into by choosing to be black. We wonder what the cost of this life story might now be.

Choosing to be black

What grief?

What spiritual abuse?

And what "therapy" might we need not simply to get over but to overcome?

Having been born like the swan that thought it was a duckling and that was negatively labeled by the ducks in the story by Hans Christian Andersen, we run the risk

Ugly duckling syndrome

of believing we are ugly. At every turn the Legion forced into our psyches and souls proclaims that we are ugliness personified: ugliness on the outside that causes others to fear us, and ugliness on the inside that causes us to be afraid. Even though our community of ugly ducklings has treasured Western middle-class values, in which work and education are synoptic gospels and Victorian respectability is a Pauline epistle, our "illegitimate" birth has required image-preserving lies and our survival of infancy has created unarticulated fears. We have become private matters gone public!

Stuck in a place where we are feared and loathed, identity-confusion is one of the ingredients of which our particular kind of ugly is made. This is something the un-ugly, who are among our most vehement abusers, fail to understand. They do not understand because they have constructed a world in which they are wanted and stimulated to build productive personalities, a world in which they have purpose and a realistic chance of realizing their Dream. The saddest thing is that our victimization makes sense to their Legion; our being psychosocially aborted and conditioned to suffer pervasive grief and bouts of depression is quite sane to them.

Victimization makes sense to the un-ugly

It is difficult to say how, but we persevere!

But as we grow older, we discover something shocking that makes our bodies ache and our souls weep with grief: we are "niggers." "Nigger" is a symbol that contradicts itself: the symbol does not tell us where it comes from, but it definitely tells us where to go: to hell! And our own African American culture teaches that this ugly needs masks, particularly masks capable of hiding our anger and rage. There is, for instance, the mask of Iceberg Slim, that master of cool who is powerful, tough, detached, and desired. So we wear the mask and are safe; but beneath our cool pose, we hunger for legitimacy.

Need for masks that are safe

Anyone should be able to see that insanity can be seductive!

The call of duty encourages us to join the military. We do not hate "the enemy"; we just hate being "niggers." But given the opportunity to fight abroad—World War I, World War II, Vietnam, Korea, Granada, Panama, the Persian Gulf—we decide that it is staying at home that might get us killed! After all, the Legion are many, and our religion has taught us a turn-the-other-cheek theology for the ugly. The theological lesson is for us to separate experience from faith: we know you are kicking and killing us, but we have undying faith that you, who stand by smiling and proclaiming love for an invisible God while visible people like us get poorer and your churches richer, will "someday" stop kicking and

Turn the other cheek theology

killing us. We also go off to fight abroad because even in our own churches and communities mere damage control rules: superficial relationships and emotional quickies are called love, but this love fails to include justice!

Feeling ugly

We return from service, having risked our lives for our country's interests, and the American people view us just the same. So we go on acting the way we feel: ugly! But we are quickly reminded by the larger society that we have the options of being ugly only towards our individual selves or towards others like us—excluding, of course, those among us belonging to the protected class who have been granted white trusteeship. At the same time, we are told within our own black communities not to counter the abuse or aggression against us with any degree of militancy, because militancy is unsafe and un-Christian.

Confrontation seen as too militant

We stop and imagine a river flowing downhill. At the top of the hill, overseers are beating and slaughtering our people. Their bodies float down river, broken and bleeding, limp and lifeless. At the bottom of the hill, black folks filled with grief collect the bodies. They bandage the broken and bury the dead. No one is encouraged or permitted to march up the hill in order to confront the slaughter, because that would be too militant and risky.

Ugly, unwanted, abused, niggerized, angry, and now enraged—we beg to die! And guess what? The person claiming to love us is the same person who threatens to 911 us!

Who is not clear about it? If one is an ugly duckling, life can be hell. And that fact alone warrants yet other masks: the passive style of coping (mask), which involves never showing any emotions that will upset anyone, rejecting spontaneity because it is too risky, intellectualizing and rationalizing all events, never sharing dreams because someone may be offended, allowing stability and consistency to pose as peace, ignoring injustice by expending enormous time and energy trying to figure out what happened and why, and connecting with powerful people who will provide protection; the "walking zombie" style of passivity (mask), where the flow of feelings is turned off but the feelings are not gotten rid of and therefore create a pressure cooker without a safety valve; the "perpetual child" style of passivity (mask), where growing up is felt to be unsafe, so that play, sex, and other forms of consumption rule the day alongside manipulation that includes stylized temper tantrums. All of these masks are the consequence of, and in turn contribute to, black grief. Can such people ever fast? Rarely, because they have holes in their souls and require more

Types of masks

Certain masks contribute to black grief

and more ingestion to give a false sense of security amid the effort merely to survive.

While part of the Legion of difficulty we face in the black church and black community is our own doing, a good measure of our grief derives from the psychological processes at work on us in the hands of the larger society. Therefore, this book will address what, psychologically and religiously, the dominant culture had to do in order to reduce our people to the point to which we succumbed to, and sometimes even accepted and promoted, our own enslavement. This question has relevance for us even today as we come to grips with the meaning and manner of black grief.

Succumbing to enslavement

When others who are not black come to understand what black grief is, they may want to say that they too have it. Perhaps they do. But we black folks are the barometers of black grief! Furthermore, the place that folk generally go when they feel black grief is the black church. The black church is not simply the place black folk go to get away from white folk who give us grief; the black church is the principal place where our culture expects us to go, even sends us, when we are suffering from black grief.

Barometers of black grief

Sitting beside us in the pews is a divorced black man, age 50, unemployed with no future goals (yet holding a

Grieving church members

graduate degree), unable to have long-term relationships with women because the relationships seem too painful, chaotic, and conflicted. Elsewhere is a black woman, age 34, college educated, a supervisor, a married mother of three children, suffering from the scars of childhood sexual abuse, and recovering from substance abuse and sexual ambivalence; a woman who works hard to hide her constant anger, including her anger toward her husband, whom she is considering divorcing. A little ways away, in a pew across the aisle, is a 28-year-old black woman, separated and single head of household, employed in a non-supervisory position with two years of college, overwhelmed by feelings of guilt, frustration, and depression; a woman who tends to become bored with good men but who is drawn to irresponsible ones because one does not have to act loving toward them when such desire is not there. Nearby is a 41-year-old separated black woman, employed in a supervisory position and holding a graduate degree; a woman who feels an emptiness that drives her to relationships in which she inevitably compromises her values for the sake of a desirable partner. A few seats down is a 41 year-old separated black man, employed in a non-supervisory position with an earned doctorate, a man who feels that his wife triggers the same negative emotions in him that his mother does, and whose professional life wearies him because, though he has followed all the rules of success, he feels he has been limited to glass-ceiling victories.

The black church is where black folks go when grief-ridden. The illusion is that the "black church" is at present anything but congregations of black people sharing common grief. To go further, the grander illusion is that the "black community" is anything but communities of black people sharing common grief. In other words, when we are all suffering the same and recognize our common suffering, we aggregate in the manner of a people. African Americans form a major symbol of the conscious and unconscious forces that make this country what it is, and our masks tie us together as a whole. But the main bond that we share is racial grief. However, aggregation around our grief is insufficient to constitute true peoplehood in the manner we romantically mean when we speak of the "black church" and "black community." True peoplehood can result only from a communal connection to our ancestral, indigenous consciousness that keeps us close to nature—its cycles of life, healing sounds and rhythms, and sacred places of retreat.

The problem, of course, does not begin with our romantic notion of the "black church." The problem is that our churches are not as healthy as we might have

Black peoplehood grief-based

True peoplehood is indigenous

Romantic notion of the black church

thought. First of all, the leadership and laity in our churches are generally unaware of the legion of grief-stricken people within; and even if the leadership and laity were aware of this extensive grief, they are generally unprepared to analyze our needs and provide the soul therapy which, in times past, was our "saving grace."

As a consequence of this lack of awareness and preparation, black folk experiencing grief, particularly those emotionally dependent on churches and pastors, often get worse rather than better; and the grief spreads like an epidemic throughout our communities. So, while the black church has been viewed as the main way-station for black folks needing healing, the deep hurt in our souls is often made deeper because we are really joining others who are not only stuck in grief-ruts but who are theologically and pastorally anesthetized. It is similar to going to the hospital because your foot hurts and awakening from the anesthesia to find that your appendix has been removed: momentarily, your foot does not hurt anymore because you are still under the anesthesia!

Emotional dependence on churches

Worst of all are those anesthetizing pastors who demand demigod-worship from their congregants and allow addictive relationships to develop with people trying to fill the holes in their souls through this kind of devotion. Some pastors may not be willing to admit it,

Demigod worship of pastors

but many know that this sort of attachment to the charisma of the clerical office can degenerate into abusive situations for women in particular, especially those for whom a favorite risk is the man of the cloth. Such women are able to go to church to get abused!

The pastors of our churches who go along with these tendencies too often permit the projection of personality and psychological isogesis to pass as truth. As in the "master" overculture, our "slave" underculture is filled with narcissistically damaged "wanabees" who are yet unhealed. In their own turn, they become black perpetrators in an increasingly victimizing subculture consumed by grandiosity and feelings of entitlement, fantasies of unlimited power and success, and insatiable desires for attention and admiration. Too often, untrained leaders are allowed to teach and preach second-rate gospel interpretations, or to claim that the death of a leader offers the only opportunity for change that is otherwise too feared or too revolutionary for those bent upon mere survival.

In this book I will be asking the Legion within the pastorate if they see any connection between the way slaves were treated and how they themselves perpetrate injustice against their own congregations, families, and communities.

Wanabee perpetrators in the church

INTRODUCTION

Black churches too often sacrifice their flocks in the name of religion to serve a psyche that has been damaged. In some cases it has been damaged because it has imbibed theologies fashioned by people dishonest about the genesis or ramifications of the Western theological heritage. This heritage considers maleness an elevating gift from God, defends the male ego as healthy and dysfunctional relationships as spiritual, justifies the abuse or destruction of anyone who openly thinks otherwise, and denigrates the great counter-hegemonic tradition found in the indigenous religious response to the master-slave dynamic of New World culture. This reality causes too many individuals within our community to oscillate between projected rage and shame-based silence.

Sacrifice of the pastoral flock

Why are we plagued with this Legion of spiritual abusers in the black church when we are already an abjectly abused people in the larger society? We are not simply members of churches in which guilt is more important than conviction, external coping behaviors more important than true changes of heart, tradition more important than identifying changes that liberate and heal, and the magic of prayer more important than proactive belief. These are only the symptoms! The problem is that we are a grieving people. And we participate in our own abuse by succumbing to those who ask us simply to

Legion of spiritual abusers

cope with our grief. And all of this grief exuding from people ugly and untouchable in our own eyes gets concentrated in the places where we gather, especially the black church.

Gospel is the blues

For this reason, we sing gospel in the black church and sing it so well: it is a form of the blues! All the symptoms are apparent: we have been experiencing unresolved grief, and we visibly are not as happy as we pretend. We drive fancy automobiles to church, wear fine clothes, and portray ourselves as successful, but the gospel singing and the preaching we listen to with varying degrees of sophistication function more as entertainment than as an authentic processing of acknowledged grief. And even those of us who acknowledge our blues, and sometimes even listen to the blues against the church's advice, think that the blues is just entertainment.

Loss of ancient healing folk-values

The sad truth is that if we tried today to rediscover those balmy singing and moaning styles that healed our indigenous grandparents and great-grandparents, many of us would find that the black community has long since discarded the best of our ancient healing folk-values for profit-making entertainment values. We are kept detached from the deeper pools of our grief, to the degree that we leave church with our grief unresolved and our lives unchanged.

INTRODUCTION

The most prominent coping mechanism in the black community is entertainment. People who cope simply wish for a better day when, by and by, things will be all right. Since enough survivors of psycho-socio-spiritual abuse trauma experience temporary relief, coping has become a legitimate cultural choice. It is further legitimized by sayings, stories, and biblical interpretations, especially from the New Testament, which support coping. While coping is a valid response in extreme situations of "desert" survival, for health's sake, one must eventually cross over out of mere coping. Coping core belief, without crossing-over core belief, results in people being unable to extricate old grief within self and community sufficiently enough to enter a new, sustainable "promised land."

Dynamics of coping

Crossing over out of coping

However, many, like Moses, have understood life as a journey full of trying processes and tough choices that lead to growth and change. Such people have understood that the ingredients of hope include a healthy faith and active participation in turning hope into reality. In fact, many of our ancestors have been of like mind, having deeply understood the intuitively-affirmed indigenous ways of preventing soul pathology, including a certain manner of singing and moaning.

Ingredients of hope

The good news is that a residue of this ancient soul

Residue of ancient soul theology

therapy remains among us. We still see it in the rhythm, tone, texture, silence, and dance of our musical affirmations and movements which invite a state of mind, body, and soul that promotes healing and harmony. This book will therefore address which aspects of a psychological and religious nature have been most soulfully therapeutic and liberating in the black experience.

The positive answer to this question lies in the manner in which we process trauma. Everyday in most of our lives, as during our legal enslavement, trauma stalks our health: natural disaster and death, physical loss and abuse, loss of property, loss of relationships, loss of position or status, loss by violence, loss of esteem by insult. When these losses mount up and trigger a domino-effect, in which one trauma tips over and knocks into another, the resulting domino-trauma uses us up. Without time or sufficient resources to heal, used-up and tired folk transmit their inadequate means of handling trauma to succeeding generations.

Stalked by trauma

Response to trauma

An inadequate handling of trauma evokes reaction rather than response. Response is positive and pro-active, while reaction is passive. The black community needs (and is capable of) the enactment of a responsive gospel, rather than an anesthetizing gospel that puts us to sleep with the sedation of coping mechanisms. We need (and have indigenous residue sufficient to re-teach us) to confront the destructive outer forces and inner voices that are causing us to grieve to death. For health's sake we must (and we can) make those forces and voices give their reasons for being before we militantly refute their "nonsense." Soul therapy will help us make the necessary gut-level changes rather than mere cosmetic improvements.

Let us not misunderstand, however. There are a Legion of forces competing against soul therapy, including the televangelistic packaging of Christianity. This form of Christianity preaches a return to narrowly focused faith, emphasizing individualism and middle-class means and attracting those whose faith allows them to exit from the presence of the less fortunate and more needy. The Legion of forces also includes the internalized Jim-Crow cultural mandates that tell us we are infected with a Hamitic color curse and therefore by divine proclamation inferior human beings—three-fifths human, in fact, by the standards of some. And perhaps the greatest force of all is that many of us do not even hear the moaning of our own souls because we are too busy pretending to be free colored facsimiles of middle-class white Americans, for whom the American Dream— a successful job and a big home in a safe neighborhood— are signs of God's favor.

Forces opposing soul therapy

Centrality of black community

A faith that is not narrowly defined, individualistic, and middle-class consumerist will emerge only when we begin to see that the center of our existence is not and should not be this one institution, the black church; but, rather, it should be the larger black community, containing variations of church and religion.

2

~ *Black Grief* ~

People can become grief-stricken simply as a result of frustrations or deprivations exceeding the limits of individual tolerance. A few common precipitating factors of grief are the loss of a loved one, loss of emotional support, and personal or economic failure. The early symptoms of grief include common emotions such as sadness, gloom, despair, anguish, tension, fear, guilt, emptiness, longing, and a lack of interest in life. Anxiety, which results from a sense of external threat to personal welfare, is another common characteristic, as is withdrawal, which protects the grief-stricken from the pain of inner feelings. Anger is often prominent too and may take the form of complaint about being unloved or mistreated, or the form of appeals for reassurance. Grief is certainly part of being human.

Precipitating factors of grief

We have equally human ways of responding to grief. In fact, the human feelings that undergird our two potential responses to grief—coping and overcoming—might even begin in the womb. Sweeten the amniotic

Two potential responses to grief

fluid, and a fetus will increase its swallowing of this fluid. At six months, a fetus has rapid-eye-movement (REM) in sleep, the kind associated with dreaming; and a fetus feels pain and responds to familiar music, soft soothing sounds producing slower heart and breathing rates. A newborn also prefer its mother's voice when it sounds more like it did in the womb. In other words, the womb can be either a nurturing place or a hostile environment; whichever predominates or impacts the unborn the most may be considered "normal" upon birth.

Generations traumatized

Imagine, then, a generation of black babies being born to traumatized mothers! Imagine many generations! Imagine the traditions or the core beliefs that could be put in motion by masters who understood or hoped that the traumatized felt normal in their victimization.

While black grief may have roots in utero, soul therapy is about creating comforting wombs and womb-like experiences that nurture rather than denature the entire person throughout her or his lifetime. Why is this so important today? Because we are still stuck in the valley of the shadow of death.

Stuck in the valley of grief

Shackled by residues of slavery, our desire for self-esteem remains unfulfilled. Being black means we have been made to lie down in the sight of green pastures; near and yet so far from still waters, with holes in our souls. The God permitted us insists we follow politically-correct paths for the majority culture's sake. Walking through the shadowy valley, we should be able to fear no evil, because we have been taught that God promised never to leave us alone. But what we understand most is the pain of the rod and staff of correction. In the presence of our enemies, we get to sit by the kitchen. We appreciate the few drops of healing oil, but our cups never overflow with anything but grief. We dream of God's providence and pray for God's justice. Yet all the days of our lives, as we have dwelled in the house of the Lord, we have never been able to afford a sovereign home of our own.

We need a physical manifestation of God, not more religious ritual or tradition! And certainly we do not need more "character-building" grief! What we need are conditions and conduits that facilitate our making it through the grief process, the valley of the shadow of death. Think of the grief process as a circle with the following stages, keeping in mind that it is difficult to separate these stages as cleanly in reality as we do in theory. Also, because grief work is rarely neat and orderly, keep in mind that a person or people can get stuck at any stage and revisit any stage; and additional trauma can restart the whole process, piling new grief upon the un-

Grief process a circle of stages

finished business of the old grief. In general, completing the cyclic stages of grief work is necessary for health and for the potential of an abundant life.

The stages of grief work are 1) shock (a temporary loss of feelings and disbelief), 2) an urge to release and express feelings, 3) depression and feelings of isolation, 4) physical symptoms, 5) fear (and the inability to think about anything but the loss), 6) guilt (things left undone and unsaid), 7) anger and resentment, 8) avoidance (resistance to reentering life and responsibilities fully), 9) a sense of hope (begins to return), 10) reality is reaffirmed (we are more durable or more delicate).

When it seems the Devil rules

In the valley of black grief—amid our shock, depression, fear, guilt, and anger—we ask ourselves where God is when the Legion is in charge. We might even wander far afield and wonder if perhaps it was the Devil who created the world and invented the concept, illusion, or mirage of God, green pastures, and still waters just to make fools of us all. Some of us, in the depths of agonizing grief, doubtless feel that we have personally met the Devil: met him just the other day and had all along been looking for a spirit instead of a person; learned too that he instinctively recognizes us as having chosen to be a people of faith raised to believe "Do not steal, Do not kill, Do not covet..."; and that he counts on us to disbelieve the mounting evidence that his ultimate goal is to consume us by causing us to get stuck in the quicksands of grief, where there can be no heaven.

Who is this Devil we have experienced in the valley of black grief? The master is always a devil to the slaves! The perpetrator a devil to his victims and his witnesses!

The demonic power of the master-slave paradigm resides, to name one count against the Devil, in the ability of individuals within the master class to amass power and wealth by harnessing and manipulating the performance power of the group. This act requires that the group produce more than it receives, and that the master receive from the group's efforts more than he himself produces. This approach to acquiring wealth in turn seduces the slaves, who up to that point had spent most of their lives working in earnest to acquire those things that make life worth living: a job, a home, security, friends, a mate, children, a decent future. Stuck in their grief because they have learned to cope rather than overcome it, those slaves dream of one day becoming masters themselves.

Master-slave paradigm

Many day-dreaming slaves of this mindset have achieved varying degrees of mastership, having found ways around the lower echelons of the multi-leveled "glass" ceiling. This slippery maneuvering is typically

Sponsor-trustee system

dependent upon the sponsor-trustee system, a modern version of the master-slave paradigm, which occurs on plantations abounding in technologies surpassing agricultural technologies of the past. The sponsor, the one who represents the majority culture, always advances the standard by which the trustee class discriminates against its own members: a black identity is permitted as long as it is mere rhetoric, for the sponsor's test of loyalty is the trustee's abandonment of indigenous identity and assumption of a persona of white privilege. The rewards for this include employment, job security, pay increases, networking creditability, and designated authority over other blacks. The sponsor also expects to be perceived and treated as superior to the trustee and his people and to be served with unquestioned loyalty.

Favored trustees with connections

Especially favored trustees are blacks in the pastorate, whose congregations benefit from their pastors' "connections." But these "connections" cost, insofar as they call for sermons on long-suffering and "waiting on the Lord," admonishments for mere coping that go by unnoticed because their sermonic delivery is stylistically perfected in the black tradition. "God blesses those who wait on the Lord," whoops the black pastor who has powerful sponsors!

Beneath the upper echelons of the glass ceiling, a

class strata is formed. In truth it is a fragmentation of the slave caste. This caste is solidified and policed to the degree that, if the lower-echelon slaves attempt politically or economically to move as a unit into the higher echelons of class and success, the trustees view this as a threat. Thus they attempt to thwart any unified upward mobility in order to keep their "petite sponsorship" intact inside the grieving black community.

Fragmentation of slave caste

This selfish maneuvering past lower-level glass ceilings which requires trustees to communicate loyalty to their sponsors by serving the needs of the sponsoring class, also requires that the sponsors' insults be silently endured. Moreover, whomever the sponsors condemn, the trustees must condemn—indeed with a greater condemnation! But as the insult becomes chronic and soul-fragmenting, grief work sooner or later leads to internalized victimization: loss of esteem (who one is), loss of worth (what one does), loss of community (where one "lives"), and loss of God's love (how one is "alive").

When insult becomes chronic

In terms of the loss of community, to mention but one dimension, the most trusted trustees become unable to recognize or greet other blacks in public because these trustees know that their special relationships with their sponsors are easily threatened by association with blacks who have not received sponsor approval. Greet-

Loss of community

ing uncleared blacks, the trustees understand, will likely give a false impression of black unity or black pride; this would not only throw into doubt the loyalty on which the sponsor-trustee relationship is based, but would bring on the illusionary threat of black power!

Internalized victimization

Once internalized victimization becomes a foundation of the slave or trustee identity, the journey to recovery is blocked, for the transformative power of grieving has been short-circuited. The consequence of short-circuited grieving is the flooding of grief across the black community. This grief flows in such abundance that it easily seeps into the black home, subverting marital relationships: demands can become excessive, possessiveness can increase, making mountains out of molehills can become an art form, seeking to control and dominate can be rationalized, and finding ways to reject others before being rejected can become undergirded by feelings of entitlement. Some grieving spouses choose to anesthetize themselves, sometimes to the degree that anything and any behavior that relieves the unhappiness becomes a medication, and always to the degree that the lives of the grief-stricken are more and more reduced to finding ways to avoid additional hurt.

The black home is also susceptible to a grief-strickenness that derives from the institutionalizing powers' defined social roles of provider and protector. The provider in American cultural tradition is the primary out-of-home supporter of the family. The ideal provider, the standard by which all other providers are judged, is white, male, educated, and wealthy. On the average, however, the provider rarely enjoys the luxury of working when and where desired; in essence, his task is a shutdown of senses, a control of emotions, a mule-like focus on work, and a sacrifice of leisure and health in pursuit of the Puritan work ethic. The provider is also expected to be a protector, which usually requires ritual demonstrations that allow loved ones to feel safe and secure. In the past such demonstrations among whites included the lynching of black men. Today, the ritual demonstrations include police brutality, the burning of black churches, other "random" acts of murder against blacks, and high-profile legal prosecution.

Provider and protector roles

Because the black woman traditionally has been mother to all children, including those of the master class, the societal apparatus has permitted her the role of family protector. On the other hand, the black man, who could not have dared act like father to the children of the master class at the risk of mutilation and death, has barely been permitted the right to father and protect his own children. And at times when the provider role for black men has been limited by social proscription, it has been difficult, especially in the shadow of the white ideal, to gain or maintain the respect of the women and children in the black community who have needed providers.

Even today, some black women believe black men should be providers and protectors equivalent to the ideal modeled by white men, and some may become upset when this does not happen. Traditionally some black men have turned to pimp and mack mentalities to compensate for their alleged provider-protector shortcomings. Their material trappings and cool pose have been admired by enough black women and children that this form of master-slave thinking has remained prevalent, even within the black church.

Whereas in white America the man rules in larger society and is provider and protector at home, that same dominant culture endorses the woman as provider and protector for the African American family. Consequently, more black women raise children alone, and more black men are incarcerated; more black women get raped, and more black men get killed.

More black men get incarcerated and killed because anger is a positive emotion only if one is the master in the master class. Only for those considered fully human is anger a healthy, natural, life-affirming reaction to the

Limits on provider role for black men

Pimp and mack mentalities to compensate

Black woman as provider-protector

Healthiness yet danger of black anger

threat against one's physical, emotional, and spiritual protective boundaries. For such people, anger communicates needs, wants, and expectations for just treatment. It often earns people in the master class, particularly men, respect, power, and safety. But the same emotion is unacceptable for people, particularly men, in the slave class. We see as evidence prisons full of such men who got angry that their protective boundaries were not simply threatened but violated.

Defending ourselves, as black men, is out of the question without the permission or assistance of the appropriate sponsor. Of course, most of the time such help is never forthcoming, for the true cause of black anger—black grief—is as illusionary to the master or sponsoring culture as it is unappreciated by our own culture. Therefore, asking for help from anyone rarely earns respect or gains assistance in matters of safety. Suppressed anger then creates rage, which involves tremendous energy. Punching a wall, breaking a taboo, or finding something or someone weaker to punish may be the next stage. Any relief experienced only gives the impression of decreasing the pain stored within, while in the meantime the grief burns destruction deeper into the soul. And there it burns, baby, burns!

Suppressed anger results in rage

These situations create fear in the black community.

Consequences of fear in the black community

Fear drives the formation of grief-ridden slave residues, those situational self-protective core beliefs that slaves originally used to survive according to specific racial etiquette but which turned into traditions separated from their original intention. Smart masters and sponsors have long realized that what slaves and trustees fear most will control their lives, and that if this fear creates self-doubt, they will behave in ways that discount their mental outputs. Self-fulfilling prophecies will then not only paint pictures of what their expectations assert, but will also determine what they are capable of believing.

Quicksands of grief

Stuck in the quicksands of this grief, many of us are reduced to thinking that life or death pivots on the question of whether one dreams of being a master or is satisfied with remaining a slave. Within this limited scope, we the grief-ridden, having no healthy means of grief resolution, bind ourselves to behaving in the diminishing manner of perpetrators, victims, and witnesses.

Perpetrators, victims, and witnesses

Perpetrators demand the approval and attention of others, deny feelings of guilt when others have a problem they contributed to, make others pay when things do not work according to their expectations, put the fear of the harm they are capable of doing in the minds of others, refuse to believe bad things are happening to others when they are, separate feelings from logic in order to avoid the sense that they support policies that victimize people, develop an all-or-none/right-or-wrong view of the world, institutionalize lies to protect personal power and privilege, make others feel more afraid or paranoid than they feel, view sex as a sovereign right, and refuse the legitimacy of others' anger. Victims feel responsible for everyone's feelings, depend on others to define them, hide anger or true feelings that might upset others, pretend that bad things are not happening when they are, keep up the appearance of being busy to avoid any real responsibility, feel afraid most of the time and find it difficult to trust others, feel that manipulation (including begging or bribery) is the best way to get what they want, feel powerless to change themselves or their situation, and feel that the rich and powerful are the most blessed. Witnesses, in a word, are victims and perpetrators waiting to happen. In the meantime, they watch (and sometimes enjoy watching) others get abused.

These traditions of abuse infect not only the black community, but the black church. Some black preachers, for instance, believe they entered the field of ministry because God called them, when actually the flocks of vulnerable sheep called them, or when actually their own history of victimization called them to be abused by parishioners for whom they are hurting, pain-ridden, burnt-

Abuse traditions in the black church

out rescuers, adjusters, placaters, and saviors. Others, including deacons, stewards, and Sunday school teachers, also compete for the number-one spot among grieving blacks, the attitude being that it beats being last in the hierarchy of grieving abusers.

When sickness sets into a church

When this sickness sets into a church, you can tell: religiously correct displays of faith become symbols of holiness and loyalty, prayers for strength become empty rituals in power-starved lives, and it becomes increasingly easy to cheat, steal, and lie. Worst of all, when this abusive tradition of perpetration and its co-dependent components of the victim and the witness get woven into the fabric of black religious experience, repentant perpetrators, victims, and witnesses find it even more difficult to ask for and receive help.

Soul drive-bys

In fact, perpetrators, victims, and witnesses can hardly break free of the sickness and become repentant because they are repeatedly brought down by the willingness of others to do soul drive-bys—and not only soul drive-bys! The violent resolution of issues of providing and protecting that inundate American culture, particularly on our television and movie screens, often causes people experiencing black grief to contemplate following suit rather than continuing to repress their gut desires. Self-hate (acceptance of the dominant culture's view of us) thus makes violent black-on-black drive-bys attractive. The fact that the dominant culture may secretly approve, makes the consequences of our self-murder less costly.

In our willingness to do soul drive-bys on each other, a behavior that may also meet dominant-culture approval, decent, hard-working, and caring black souls are being shot to pieces for any number of personal reasons, such as black folks hating to see others in the community do well. Some of us take little responsibility for our decisions, yet want the world, including other struggling black folk, to pay for our unhappiness. Some of us who do not work or go to school, and yet demand to be taken care of, feel justified in raging against those who do get an education and who do work. In fact, the energy some of our soul gangsters put into destroying the hearts of others truly amazes: such energy and commitment is absent when it comes to personal growth and community-building.

Raging against one another

Another kind of soul drive-by results from passive-aggressive strategies, in which compliance is feigned, while aggression subtly predominates. This life-saving response to slave captivity, which turned into a slave residue, has been passed down and transformed into tradition (and mistaken for positive African American culture). From this tradition derives the art of "acting nice"—

Passive-aggressive strategies

smiling in a person's face while actually disliking them and perhaps also maliciously talking behind that person's back. We find both of these traditions in the black church, and both of them are destructive soul drive-bys.

In addition to our willingness to do drive-by name-calling, backstabbing, gossiping, and to call upon white sponsors and their institutional apparatuses to participate in the soul assassinations, we put our personal hatreds before white America. We do so not only on television talk shows, but on the job, on the yard, in the streets, and in the courtrooms. Too many black women, in airing their personal sexual business before the whole world on television and in music, no longer wish to be thought of as ladies. They have not learned from doggish black men who boast about how many women they have slept with and how much they can hurt them, that this entertainment does nothing to build black self-esteem or gain the respect of other groups.

On top of this, the black comedic desecration of black mothers and motherhood has found an acceptable artistic means of expressing and capitalizing on our internalized victimization. Just as a diet of word-images with healthy meanings connect to the physical reality of the body, the emotional reality of the mind, and the ultimate reality of the spirit, words like "nigger," "motherfucker," and

Airing dirty laundry

Unhealthy word-images

"bitch" comprise a diet of images that bring more spiritual heartburn to the black community.

Again, the broader American context of master and slave or sponsor and trustee doubtless has influenced our willingness to kill each other's souls. When slaves or trustees succumb to the games of masters or sponsors, they do so in some cases on the hope of simple survival, since living life fully is a restricted option or an outright unattainable goal. In the face of the resulting self-denial, mutual rejection, and sense of isolation, a fear-based drive for acceptance in the broader scheme arises. This drive can be so strong that the slaves or trustees try to reduce their personal pain through a revised image of acceptability while simultaneously seeking revenge against the idea itself of being unwanted, untouchable, and "ugly": they join the masters or sponsors in injuring other blacks. This strategy of survival, for those who simply want to keep their bodies alive with as little threat and discomfort as possible, permits the slaves or trustees abused by whites to justify abusing blacks when they themselves rise to "petite" ruling situations.

Succumbing to the master's game

Survival strategies do not always involve such seemingly complex ideas as spiritual drive-bys. They also include familiar phenomena such as consumerism, which is a survival strategy that creates grief-ridden distinctions

Survival strategies

between haves and have-nots. Consumerism contrasts with "living strategies" that involve an overall spirit of sharing and a balance between what is produced and consumed. While survival strategies involve the now, living strategies are about the past, present, and future in sync, where past plantings grow in the present and can be faithfully expected to yield harvest when needed in the future. Mere survivors, identifiable by a rampant consumerism, get caught in the now and experience only repetition—more of this, more of that—without growth. Those who are alive with living strategies, however, understand planting, growing, and harvesting to be an ongoing cycle with empowering rites of passage. With mere survival strategies of a consumerist type, notions of black racial unity and justice are mere wishes without hands and feet, because the resources with which to create the necessary shared reality—time, thought, energy, and money—are being squandered on lesser needs.

Living strategies versus survival strategies

While I have been suggesting that some of our grief is self-created or at least self-perpetuated, I want to say more about the relationship between our well-being and what people think, feel, and say about us. Words and concepts are forms of image, and images, which hold meaning, can trigger symptoms of dis-ease in us. Mother's womb, the womb called family, and the wombs

External and self-perception and well-being

called church and community, all include seeds of thought and concept whose vitality and potentiality (or lack thereof) are dependent on control of the soil into which the seeds must be planted. Our traditional victimizers understand that properly seeded and reinforced, the basic assumptions and ideas upon which everyday slave or trustee thought and action are based become predictable and perpetual. Therefore, considerable effort has been expended to make certain that the thought-seed images that sprout into our core beliefs are riddled with deprecating self-images and negative self-references. This is for the purpose of producing or perpetuating the caste that remains to this day an active casualty of the Africa-to-America chattel-slavery holocaust.

The resultant black grief affects the energy and infects the intellect we direly need in order to discover what types of thought-seed image and soil we actually possess. Without the energy and intellect, our awareness is reduced to cognizance of everything but the grief itself. When the capacity and ability to explore awareness is limited, our choices are then decreased, our grief increases, and our identity begins to change because our view of the world is challenged to the degree that its content is changed. On top of that, hidden within grief are fears that encourage us to go on living life as if this loss of self

Grief affects energy and infects intellect

never occurred, and this causes us to stumble on blindly into valley after valley of self-esteem traps. The results can be devastating: a psychic and soul sickness that passes from one generation to the next and in each new generation the unresolved grief assassinating potential as if the trauma had just transpired yesterday.

Healthy self-esteem and grief-resolution

On the other hand, the process of grief-resolution can end suffering when we possess healthy self-esteem. Healthy self-esteem allows us to trust our minds and judgments and to enjoy exercising our ability to think. Without it, we become mentally passive, live in a world of limited awareness, and become less tolerant of difficulties. But while healthy self-esteem is life-supporting and life-enhancing, poor self-esteem poisons life and deals in death because it makes giving up easier to justify.

Healthy core belief

Healthy core belief, on which healthy self-esteem rests, has uncountable blessings. It allows us to adapt to various situations with self-control; to develop and maintain a continuing sense of security despite hardships and traumatic change; to keep a sense of our own unique identity and purpose; to develop and maintain a sense of confidence and safety that makes possible positive humor and comfortable relationships with others; to feel a sense of "OK-ness" when alone; to have a balanced day-to-day lifestyle and effectiveness in independent or cooperative roles; to experience happiness along with the ability to compete where appropriate and compromise without feeling undone; to possess feelings of empowerment that support our ability to affirm our gender, ethnicity, and peculiar personhood, and still be other-centered and giving of self; to develop and maintain dependability without being rigid; to develop and nurture a positive sense of relationship to God and God's creation, however stated or envisioned.

As a people trapped in conflicting core beliefs, however, we are now hardly qualified to be our own caregivers. At worst we do not even like to face or discuss the idea that we are, as individuals and as a people, grief-stricken, let alone the idea that perhaps our religion has betrayed our health. At best we are too slow in identifying unhealthy core belief and displacing it with revitalized core belief that promotes wholeness and emotional balance and, in turn, enables us to function at full capacity intellectually, emotionally, physically, and spiritually. Somewhere in the middle, neither worst nor best, we simply have no cultural definition of health. We have learned simply to inhale the ether of psychological unhealth which poisons our perspectives on what is therapeutic for our souls in a society that does not love us and in communities in which we ourselves have chosen not to love one another.

Trapped in conflicting core belief

Pretense of love and truth

Blind to the blessings of being in search of healing love, we have learned to place so-called peace before truth and thus have chosen to be people of the lie. The pretense of love and truth, a culture-bound immuno-depressant disorder we inherited from our masters and sponsors, means that the very institution we think should relieve us of our grief is actually giving us grief. The chronic avowal of innocence or unawareness with regard to spiritual abuse in the black church means that our urge to maintain the status-quo has produced shame and guilt instead of life-changing conviction. Cautious in liberating declarations as well as delinquent in manifestations of love, we find that the disorder at hand causes hypocrisy that stagnates every effort to express the prophetic truth that could lead to real and lasting love and peace. Worst of all is that we in the black church are allowing ourselves to sink into a dense, multi-layered bondage in which no one is permitted to talk about the real causes of our dis-ease.

Crying does not help anymore. While resolution of grief is aided by the acknowledgment of others that loss is real, unacknowledged grief is now our bitter reality. Even those who are responsible for our loss claim it to be an illusion and thus create a situation in which the loss becomes more traumatic. And when loss becomes more traumatic, people are more easily stranded in the grief-process and soon exhausted. Unappreciated grief also leads people to suppress their "unacceptable feelings"; and once they are numb to feelings associated with grief, people find that their capacity for contentment and joy is diminished. A person may then become so rational that feelings do not matter, or become so emotional that rationality does not make any sense. The rational reaction may cause a person to opt for living in an emotional coma and ignoring or minimizing feelings while seeking to "fix the problem." The emotional reaction may cause a person to "need the feelings fixed" before any problem can be resolved.

Unappreciated grief

Our "keep silent" commandment in the black church, the commandment that cancels out all other Commandments, permits our grief to fester and thrive; and too much grief contains shame. While guilt results from doing, shame results from being; once shame is internalized, it is characterized by a psychic numbness that becomes the foundation for a soul murder which conditions every single relationship in our lives. To compensate for the powerful pervasiveness of shame, people develop false selves, such as the falsity of always being cool. While false selves shelter people from the pain of their inner lonely selves, they diminish or destroy our human ability to grieve and get through the grief process.

Keep silent commandment

Safeguarding the inner-self

The problem with the "cool pose," as a way of defending the sense of self, begins when the original reason for the defense mechanism is lost, and the response becomes reflexively self-sustaining and subsequently necessary for survival. Slaves who understood this pose to be a put-on to fool the master, or to be a temporary means of safeguarding the essential inner-self while giving of the external self, could remove the pose when it was no longer necessary or when health required its removal so that accumulated suffering and anger could be released. But when the cool pose became a way of life or style, our problem began.

Cool pose of hip-hop and gangsta generation

For instance, the youth of today's hip-hop generation, trustees of a sort uniquely their own, believe their cool pose to be therapeutic black expression. In reality, this slave residue holds them enthralled to trauma-response. Youths of the "gangsta" mentality have a cool pose that is even more hardened because it results from the warrior phenomenon. In the urban or industrial environment, as in the previous agricultural environments, protecting requires size, strength, and an adequate warrior mentality. Except in the heat of protecting, warriors are compelled to control their emotions and to hide their fear while exemplifying courage. Surviving battles and wars intact, while hiding fear and vanquishing the enemy, brought honor and prestige. Even the warrior who fought on the losing side was honored if cool to the end. Thus the cool pose, even for "the defeated" (which is what today's tough black youths are), provided the appearance of the warrior mentality.

In the black church, the cool pose takes the form of "acting white"—that is, worshiping in a controlled, unemotional manner. This form might have been good strategy when the master was watching in order to eradicate every vestige of African indigenousness, but when the put-on invaded autonomous black space, the resultant "tradition" of stoicism interfered with our being able to "let it all go" in the face of loss. "Having church" has traditionally meant letting go until you get happy, an important step in the process of grief-resolution. The soul suffering from grief needs to be able to cry and cry out in a safe and supportive environment. This catharsis helps keep anger manageable. The avoidance of feelings is also the avoidance of our spiritual depths, and I do not mean those feelings that are part and parcel of the entertainment value in black worship: gospel-singing, dancing, whooping, and shouting disconnected from their genesis in grief-resolution.

Cool pose in the black church

When a supportive environment is available in church, the continuation of the grief process goes largely unsupported outside of the church. When family members and friends "shush" people suffering from loss or legitimate rage by telling them to "be strong," they are sometimes short-circuiting necessary expressions of grief. Still others, bringing evangelical beliefs with them into family and community settings, may dismiss grief-caused illness as the work of the Devil or evil forces. Such messages could leave younger recipients trapped between real spiritual needs and religious/doctrinal requirements.

Short-circuiting expressions of grief

The problem with our business-as-usual, shame-driven soul drive-bys is that our self-inflicted insults stack up and become chronic. As our grief work becomes more difficult, complicated by everything else going on in our grief-ridden lives, feelings of victimization—fear, anger, guilt, self-pity, and more shame—stampede over our self-image. Meaning itself, via the vehicle of remembering, then becomes a dead-end street. At this point there is little, if any, affirmation of what previously has been good, because the capacity to appreciate what remains has been diminished. When the transforming power that comes from moving through the grief process is completely blocked, the ability to shift from feelings of limitation to thoughts of possibility disappears. Unresolved past grief next contaminates the present sense of self by activating inner voices that say we do not deserve things, and this

Unresolved grief

restricts future potential. Because belief about the future affects inner-drive and motivation, if we believe that the future holds only condemnation for us, we will often behave in ways that get us condemned. Or, if we believe that the future will be full of anger and violence, we will often behave in ways that generate such emotions. So the past plays an important part in the resolution of present grief, which is why grief-resolution can be both near and far away.

In a life driven by such mounting pain, avoiding pain can easily become the object of survival. Fighting, withdrawing, pretending, denying, and diverting become some of the tools used for scaling the rough side of the mountain. Or we face the opposite phenomenon of glamorizing the grief by, let us say, "waiting to exhale." In a world where loss of self-esteem cycles and recycles without a script, holding on to grief becomes a way of relating to the world. Being viewed as unacceptable, undesirable, unsuitable, unattractive, unbecoming, unpleasant, unapproachable, disagreeable, inappropriate, contaminated, debauched, savage, profane, fringe, marginal, intrusive, offensive, transgressive, taboo, frightful, hideous, obnoxious, and monstrous becomes a way of getting attention! But this merely results in more grief for those of us who are participants in a culture that has lost

Avoiding or glamorizing grief

its ability to complete the grieving process.

Passing grief on to children

We can almost anticipate the sudden fall that will hurl us downward, causing grief-inflicting injury upon our future generations of children. In effect, their childhoods become crushed; and they experience a loss of freedom to make mistakes, a loss of the option to question authority, a loss of the opportunity to complete grief-cycles, a loss of the capacity to trust the products of their emerging minds, a loss of the ability to enjoy thinking and producing instead of consuming the thought and produce of others, and a loss of the trust of others that is necessary to live fully and heal from insult.

Grief a parasite on black culture

Some of us know these things all too well and must be wondering if grief is not simply inherent to black culture. The truth is, grief is a weed grown up within our culture's garden. Therefore, we must scrutinize who we are at the level of our core beliefs, because our grief can be worked through only at the root of those beliefs. If our core beliefs can be purged of all the unhealthy seeds and parasites, many of which originate from varying degrees of cultural adherence to the master-slave and sponsor-trustee systems, release, renewal, and an end to our suffering will come. From then on, our daily recovery from loss will be an opportunity for upward spiritual growth rather than cliff-fallen demise. This is easier said than done, of course, because scrutinizing who we are also requires scrutinizing who we once were.

The greatest obstacle to the resolution of our grief is not that our clergy are alone ill-prepared to do all this necessary scrutinizing. Rather, we have been unable, except in times of intolerable persecution or unprecedented group opportunity, to come together as a people to improve our collective condition. The reason is that we are not as much a people as we have presumed. We have spent more time building up the black church rather than the black community. Today, we have historic and prestigious churches but do not see their counterparts in our communities. What we share in common (and even that sharing has differentials) is the experience of being unwanted, untouchable, and ugly-ducklings—in a word, black grief.

A people only in shared grief

However, our indigenous forebears, who shared the common roots of oral tradition, were far more a people in the sense that no one had to grieve alone. While our indigenous ancestors' right to define themselves might have been in the possession of the slave masters, their spirituality brought together a core belief that made hope possible in the face of daily impossibilities. This indigenous spirituality was nurtured in the context of the village, in which shared core beliefs and connected patterns

Indigenous spirituality and village

of conduct undergirded a support system that allowed for clarity of identity and mutual trust.

Today, our "village" is anywhere our families live, our culture thrives, and black people receive help in acquiring not merely the material requisites for survival but also those essential, immaterial values that are transferred through personal, family, and community relationships. The leadership of the black church is essential here. Black church leadership can help the black family and community work together to make the village a place where life is consistent and dependable; where needs are fulfilled; where people are committed, incorruptible, empathetic, and full of hope; where improvement is rewarded; where autonomy is accommodated; where anger is healthy; where hostility in the world is real but, by design, diffused in a truly loving environment; where parenting deficiencies are countered and the growth of children is encouraged; where people will not feel alone in bearing their reality; and where a sense of hope and the feeling of support will make the resolution of grief more successful and permanent. Harmonious village relationships with self, others, the community, and a providential God are the basis of the therapeutic tradition of soul therapy which can keep our souls renewed daily.

Ideals of village life

3

~ *Spiritual Abuse* ~

Anyone wishing to reduce African people to chattel and make these indigenous people accept their status as ugly property, sooner or later would have to figure out an essential step: how to restructure every element of their existence through strategies and techniques designed to thwart every indigenous effort to maintain or repossess the right to define their own being. On top of that, theology, the rational study of God and God's creation, would have to be employed as a foundational and final prism through which slavery would be justified and white guilt ameliorated. Psychology would have to team up to communicate approved racist attitudes among whites, and core beliefs that promoted wholeness and emotional balance among blacks would have to be poisoned at every turn; for slave mental processes could not operate independent of chattel management, whose effort at all times would be to make slaves function at the fullest capacity physically but not intellectually, emotionally, or spiritually.

The processes would include the necessary renaming

Reducing a people to chattel

Renaming in the chattelization process

of the slave with a "Christian name" or, at the very least, a name to the master's liking. The renaming ritual would be an opportunity for the master to hold class before the other slaves on what it means to be a "good nigger." Because a name represents elements of a person's humanity that bestows identity and worth, this tradition of renaming would help the mantle of slavery pass from generation to generation. Eventually it would get to the point where the enslaved would simply rename themselves.

But even the long-term effects of renaming could not alone bring about the desired objectives of those wishing to make indigenous people accept their status as ugly property; for the "unconverted slave," the one who remained indigenous to the end, would be an ever-present part of and influence on the slave community. Resistance to the conversion or training process under example of the unconverted slave would range from outright rebellion and insurrection to passive-aggressive slow-downs of work and property damage. For the masters to overcome this still persistent indigenousness, an indigenousness naturally spiritual and nurturing of the divine within human character, any and every strong medicine would be necessary.

Ever-present resistance of unconverted slave

One such medicine used to break and remake the indigenous slave was terrorism of the kind dramatized in the television movie, *Roots*. In this movie, Kunta Kinte was abused, violated, and tortured, but the observing slaves were terrorized. The immediate objective of terrorism would be to make the slaves comply passively to the master's every wish and whim, but one of the most important objectives would be to make self-knowledge so painful within the slaves that forms of identity-denial were necessary for psychological survival.

Torture and terrorism

Should there be success in all this, the right of black people to define themselves would be the property of the white culture, according to the trinity of the white-God/white-savior/white-master. Unfortunately, there was success. And the entire process of making Africans accept their status as ugly property was not simply abusive; it was spiritually abusive to a people deeply spiritual.

Here I intentionally use the term *spiritual*, as opposed to *religious*. The two words, *spiritual* and *religious*, are often used interchangeably, but the concepts are as different as the Bible's references to love and respect: spirituality would be the equivalent of love and religiosity the equivalent of respect. To be religious is to be engaged in the interpretation of the unknown, the control of the uncontrollable, the personification of human ideals, the projection of human meanings and social patterns into the ultimate. This naturally involves

Spiritual versus religious

the integration of culture and the ultimate legitimization of social systems. To be religious, then, means to be part of a cultural phenomenon comprised of shared meanings that help people make choices, interpret events, plan actions, and determine whether behavior is good and desirable or bad and to be avoided.

On the other hand, to be spiritual means to tap into the full range of consciousness—the rational, emotive, and intuitive in concert—as this consciousness plumbs the phenomenal, deep, energetic, eternal aspects of daily life. If we understand people to be essentially spiritual beings having human experiences and know that abuse is improper treatment, then spiritual abuse results from any consistent pattern where people in need of help, support, or greater empowerment of their deep, energetic, eternal parts are victimized in a manner that results in the weakening of their spiritual vitality. Spiritual abuse is also abuse of God; for if we are born "children of God," then what are we when we become mature?

The process of making black people accept their status as ugly property fits neatly into this category of spiritual abuse. Does this surprise us? While we have little problem conceiving of slavery and racism as affecting our secular or material lives, past and present, we have difficulty thinking of slavery and racism as having affected our

Spiritual abuse

spiritual lives. We acknowledge the effects of racism in the raging battle over the secular education currently being proffered in most American schools, yet we fail to grasp the original and on-going effect of slavery and racism on the spiritual life, including how the psychological effects of forcing ugly status on us has influenced the self-abusing education and religion we now so readily accept.

One reason chattelization and racism continue to strike at us spiritually is that "we the people"—the American populace—have chosen not to love universally. First of all, "we" have never agreed on a definition of love that includes justice, opportunity, and security for all. Instead, America has invested so much in building a society around core belief which is the antithesis of love that narcissistic insults licensed by American culture make even the desire to love us too complex!

American society's choice not to love

This licensing of insult derives from core belief that is learned during the process of socialization, which means that the beliefs most sedentary and understandings most plausible to subsequent generations of Americans are likely to be those previously held by the group and modeled by people especially important to the group. Culture, then, is comprised of people and groups who carry the past—even an oppressive past—with them through the intergenerational transferral of core belief. Of course,

Core belief and culture

people can reject or modify core belief communicated and modeled and passed on by the group, such as the core belief that undergirded chattelization and racism; but all core belief gains stability and effectiveness by its inculturalization, which in turn makes difficult any extrication of that core belief from collective and individual identity. Why is this? Because core belief makes sense of identity and social being.

Racism and religion

We cannot deny the fact, then, that exclusionary core beliefs have cohabited and produced such contradictory offspring as the union of racism and religion, a union so culture-syntonic that even the two great commandments of Jesus were prostituted in the name of God and country to make the hatred of black people as American as mom and apple pie. The consequence of the cohabitation and prostitution is that too many whites still participate in denying us certain inalienable rights: the right to hold a secure belief in our own value, the right to be "pro-self" without being tagged anti-other, the right to give self-actualization needs a high priority, the right to nourish relationships beyond the limits of color. Because of this reality, all the national covenants instructing "we the people" to act as though we love one another are difficult to implement and virtually impossible to sustain.

SPIRITUAL ABUSE

Why is it that the two great commandments of Jesus were so easily prostituted to make the hatred of blacks as American as mom and apple pie? One reason is that America was colonized by Europe's cursed and victimized. Having gained power without first having been healed, these people have ever since felt normal in victimizing others.

Those of us black folks who do not understand this relationship bear the brunt of the most enduring and sadistic of "mom and apple pie" jokes: being invited to participate in the immigrants' Dream, only to find our very sleep thwarted before we reach REM. To put it differently, every time we have attempted to submit our ticket to the Dream show, the ticketeers at the box office inform us that our particular admittance is not for the day's showing. This box-office behavior is backed by a standard message of the white church which is a combination of salvation talk and the Protestant work ethic, and which is intended to placate us and prevent us from protesting against the box-office gatekeepers. Decoded, the message means that we are to take our racially flawed and physically feared selves and return to the back of the line, where we are to wait, keep slaving, and be patient until the powers that be decide to modify the system gradually.

Dreams deferred

The fact that America's former immigrants had been the rejects of European society did not prevent them from becoming rejecters of others. Instead, they became newly minted perpetrators of an American caste system based on race, as well as breakers of treaties and destroyers of indigenous peoples. The materialization of American slavery, in which the dynamics of chattel-making were woven intractably into the psyche of the emerging national culture, meant that the racial "ism" did not develop by accident but by the comfortable marriage of prejudice to power and purpose. The prejudice was the viewing of people of color as ugly ducklings. The power was money, business ownership, community status and reputation, information, and the gun. The purpose was to reduce Africans to chattel, refuse them the right to resist their oppression in the same manner as the colonists had resisted theirs by the colonial powers, and to guard and control all the gates to power henceforth and forevermore.

In other words, a complex array of cooperating bio-psycho-social systems had to be in place; and these systems, once imposed upon every sector of the slaves' reality, would eventually make it natural for the slaves, even when they became ex-slaves, to participate in their own victimization. For this process to have unfolded, however, master and slave or sponsor and trustee, and their respective have and have-not cultures had to become co-dependents: the master class had to create, internalize, and propagate a theology that slaves were helpless; and the slaves had to imbibe the belief that their requirements for survival would be taken care of by the earthly-appointed source of goods.

Master-slave co-dependency

This master-slave system permeated all levels of life within and without the slave community, during and beyond actual physical chattelization. Just as the slave community could be prevented from adequately perceiving and thereby meeting the needs of its members, for instance, so could a slave parent be prevented from adequately perceiving and thereby meeting the needs of her child; and likewise could the culture-sensitive institutions of larger society be set up so that black people at the micro level of family and mezzo level of community could not have their needs met in all but narrowly prescribed ways, lest those ways be labeled illegal, unpatriotic, or un-Christian. Similarly, just as the slave community could be controlled in how it communicated its discomforts or fears to its members in nonverbal ways, so could a slave parent be controlled in how she communicated her discomforts or fears to the infant in nonverbal ways; and likewise could the culture-sensitive institutions

Master-slave system

of larger society be controlled so that black people at the micro level of family and the mezzo level of community were limited in the ways they could communicate their discomforts and fears in nonverbal ways. Or, just as a psychology could be engendered in which unconscious hostility was a part of the nonverbal and proverbial communication among the members of the slave community, so could a psychology be engendered in which unconscious hostility was communicated either nonverbally or proverbially in the parent-child relationship; and likewise could a psychology be engendered in which unconscious hostility would be part of the communication culture of the "slave" community (media coverage, education, and so forth).

America a dysfunctional culture

In sum, America had become a culture of narcissists, a dysfunctional culture, and also a shame-based culture. Over this lurked the shadowy fear that what America was sowing would one day have to be reaped. America had also become an addictive culture and a co-dependent culture. The development of a culture among slaves and their descendants that participated in this addiction to the white American culture, exemplified by co-dependent relationships, was a major consequence of the American chattel system.

We can better understand this particular level of co-dependency if we think of it on the level of interpersonal relationships. Co-dependents—usually good volunteers, servers, and sufferers—are devoted to taking care of and making themselves indispensable to others: "Oh I can't go out of town this week, the church would be absolutely nowhere without me." Co-dependents usually work and take care of others to the point that they themselves develop all kinds of physical, emotional, and spiritual problems. They also love to be in relationships with addicts of one sort or another. And because they want to be liked, loved, and respected, they are unable to tell when they are being deceived by these addicts. This sort of behavior is exactly what black co-dependency with the master class amounted to during slavery.

Co-dependent behavior

Our co-dependency under American chattelization resulted in one irrefutable reality: we learned how to suffer exceptionally well. We are so good at suffering that movies about our suffering turn us on! Our comedians know we like to laugh about our suffering, so that is what the Home Box Office (HBO) has on for us to watch. We love to suffer so much that we make each other suffer. And then we require all manner of fantasy religions to hide this reality from us—that is, religions that deny the relevance of experience to faith. But unresolved grief can kill! And without healing, unresolved

Romance of black suffering

grief kills God-given potential, for it dooms many of us to living life at the Cross and worshiping a crucified but unresurrected Jesus.

Our co-dependency as suffering servants also has us supplying the needs of the master culture, to the exclusion of our own more immediate needs, by causing us to function as a consumer culture. At one time, the black community was more aware of the psychological and spiritual paradox under which we lived. Now, in an attempt to avoid, deny, and escape our grief, many of us unconsciously seek the temporary high that consumerism and conspicuous consumption give. Our suffering even feels better for the moment; but once the excess has been digested, more and more is needed for us to feel full and good again: more fancy automobiles, more fine clothes, more flashy jewelry. Sounds like pimps; I would never want that description to sound like regular church folk or preachers!

Temporary high of consumerism

At some point, consumer-hungry black folk will also experience the invisible barriers that separate us from the most fulfilling goods and excess, and more grief will result when we try to hold on to things that are not in our possession or within our reach. This very phenomenon is typical in an abusive system: getting people to treat such lower needs as consumerism as their higher needs,

Lower versus higher needs

SPIRITUAL ABUSE

higher even than spiritual pursuits and well-being.

So, the master-slave culture of the United States produced the obvious: a master culture unwittingly dependent on a slave culture, a slave culture made dependent on a master culture, and pathological co-dependency posing as love. Narcissism and pathological co-dependency went hand in hand, in other words; and even today, cultures that choose to build on forced lies run the risk of producing more evil than good.

For the hard-core narcissists, this master-slave culture has produced only two types of people: those who are like them (extensions of their ego and power), and those who are not like them (inferior and necessarily neutered). When we ask individuals within the narcissistic culture to declare the subject of their love and spell diversity, in their hearts they answer: "Just me," which is spelled 'me, myself, and I.'" When we ask a whole community within the narcissistic culture to declare the subject of their love and spell diversity, inside they answer: "Just us, which is spelled 'only those who are like us.'" When we ask people within the narcissistic culture who claim to follow Christ to define love and spell diversity, inside they too answer: "J-e-s-u-s, which means 'Just us.'" That is their form of justice.

Just us versus justice

This means that, in white hands, Christianity is too

Christianity in white hands

often a narcissistic religion catering to the psychological need of fearful and insecure people who want to appear sure and superior, people who have become afraid as a response or reaction to losing themselves totally in what they fear. Life-changing conviction cannot exist when whites fear life without privilege and presume privilege to be their protector. Fear lies at the heart of abuse. Unfortunately, it is the American majority, involved in its "just-us" pursuit of privilege without the sacrifice of personal pain, whose fear-inspired world views define for us and disperse to us what is called Christian love. This dispersement, in particular, is spiritual abuse!

Power behind cultural narcissism

The power behind cultural narcissism are the educational, economic, psychological, and theological forces that unite racism and religion. Education includes not only what is taught, but when people are taught, where they are taught, how they are taught, and who is allowed to teach what is taught. Psychology involves what people must do to have self-image (self-esteem and self-worth), when people are considered normal or good, where people are allowed to have needs met, how people are named or classified, and what groups of people are considered fully human. Economics involves what people are considered worthy of hire, where people are allowed to work or make a living, how people are treated while on the job, and when people are hired and fired. Theology involves what God is like in relationship to people, when and where God is believed to be moving and not moving on behalf of people, how people approach God or their relationship with God, and what people are considered children of God.

The union of educational, economic, psychological, and theological forces in the service of uniting racism and religion has been so complete that the marriage of prejudice to power, with specific plans and strategies for maintaining dominance and privilege over blacks, has been defended by many whites as both American and Christian. Abusers naturally expect the system to protect them!

With narcissism canonized in this fashion, emancipation could not possibly mean that blacks would be able to enjoy the rights and privileges of whites, that they would be party to the control of and protection by the state, that they would be granted key positions in organizations, and that they would have equal access to wealth. Even those whites who opposed slavery had already been deputized to maintain the system, so as not to have to relinquish either their sense of unique racial status, or their various privileges and prerogatives. Spiritually abused and cut off from economic opportunities

Canonization of narcissism

and political representation, most ex-slaves spiraled into poverty, disease, and spiritual slumber. This grief set us up to become the convenient scapegoats for not only our own lack of collective progress but for everything presumed to have gone wrong in America.

Today we have not only romanticized our institutionalized victimization, sometimes using Christian imagery, but we have also given in to the unrelenting pressures of the chattelization process and its intergenerational "trauma gifts" of the Africa-to-America psycho-spiritual sojourn. To be sure, it is a sad thing to see healthy indigenous human beings, once the proud possessors of great cultural traditions and achievements, reduced to Sambos, Uncle Toms, Aunt Jemimas, and Tobys. We vilify the Uncle Tom in our rhetoric but offer him as a pragmatic role model; for, although we know who has and who continues to enforce policies that destroy our children's chances of realizing their fullest potential in life, we yet speak of loving our enemies not as a strategy but as a way of life: "Leave evil be; by and by it will destroy itself."

Intergenerational trauma gifts

The power to perform spiritual abuse against us proved seductive and even erotic to some whites; eventually, television and cinema became vehicles for the perpetration. The man on the screen working in behalf of

Seductiveness of spiritual abuse

whites, traditionally the man in white or wearing a white hat, is the good guy and hero. Blacks, like American Indians, are savages, in the same fashion that women of any group are fair sexual game. Savages are romanticized only when they are good to the whites or to their interests—Pocahontas, Gunga Din, Uncle Tom.

An example of how the needs of narcissistic whites were satisfied in a manner entertaining to them but spiritually abusive to blacks is that famous dramatized form of the white Jesus: Tarzan. Tarzan was created to celebrate the virtues of the civilized white and the converse lack of virtues in the African inhabitants of the so-called "Dark Continent." In the movie and television series, a white baby raised by an ape grows up to be the "king of the jungle" and as a full-grown man is more intelligent and moral than all the indigenous people put together. How demeaning to the self-esteem of black people to be told that even a white person raised by a subhuman species is innately superior to them.

Tarzan

The Africans in the *Tarzan* series were also depicted as people engaged in ancestral worship, animism, and superstition, rather than worship of the one true God. But such propaganda, which met the psycho-spiritual and social needs of whites by openly supporting a bias against anything good coming out of Africa, ignored the evi-

Bias against anything good out of Africa

dence that traditional African religions were based on the belief of a Supreme Being. This God was so singularly providential and so interwoven into daily life that there could be no separation of religion from culture or the sacred from the profane. By ignoring these facts and believing the worst, the European ego was stroked and the discriminatory social order affirmed. Yet curiously, even as African culture was being distorted and African self-esteem crushed in order to relegate a people from that continent to permanent chattel status, this claim of Christian love for the victims still remained. The reality is that the master-slave cultural paradigm of narcissistic perpetrator and passive victim has actually made co-dependency and mutual addiction the substitute for Christian love.

Pledge of innocence about racism

With few exceptions, the white church is the paradigm of the pretense of love. Its chronic pledge of innocence with regard to systemic racism is so transparent that the predominance of shame-producing guilt over life-changing conviction is readily visible to anyone who is honest. We are left only to marvel at how well people can lie so passionately and love simultaneously.

This behavior is not new. We just do not like to discuss it! But we can no longer run from the truth simply because whites do not want to hear it, or because we want to be sensitive to their needs, or because we are afraid. The truth is, unchallenged abuse too easily turns into efforts to dominate in order to avoid anticipated domination, efforts to humiliate in order to avoid anticipated humiliation, and efforts to deprive others in order to avoid anticipated deprivation.

Truth unchallenged

White America and its white religion have participated in our destruction, and they have done so while yet claiming to be righteous purveyors of the Christian love ethic. This reality should tell us that we cannot cave in to the pattern of belief that mandates our powerlessness and then calls it a crime to fight back against abuse. Let us be starkly aware that, as we waste time debating among ourselves on the merits of fighting back, the culture-bound immuno-depressant disorder that plagues whites with the most extreme of contradictions continues to mutate, thrive, and victimize us unmercifully with a spiritual terrorism that produces in us post-traumatic stress responses.

Post-traumatic stress responses

These responses in turn produce institutionalized revictimization in our communities: ministers and congregations seldom being held accountable for theologies and behaviors that promote individualism and materialism over restorative justice and community responsibility; ministers womanizing, chasing children of both sexes, embezzling resources, growing wealthy while the masses struggle; church members enjoying mess and willing to destroy a pastor who cannot deal with their mess; and black congregations caring little for others outside their memberships or circles of church friends. Against this Legion of powers and principalities we currently have no good defense. As Jim Crow captives, psychologically blinded about who we are, we have been weakened by spiritual sabotage to our sense of self.

Constantly reminded of who has personal authority over us—and thus pressured to be preoccupied with obedience, performance, and submission to unspoken rules about which we usually learn only after we break them—our souls are embattled and traumatized, and we are frightened, secretive, and full of shame. The weapon of humiliation, as in the genre of the Tarzan fantasy, has made us image-conscious to the point that now the mere look of being blessed is more important than its actual state, the appearance of truth is more important than an actual truth that could set us free, and the pretense of loving is more palatable than love itself. Terminally allergic to the invading insults from the white world outside, we permit our deeply ingrained self-hate to go unnoticed and fester.

The fact that we can now assault, rape, rob, and mur-

Weapon of humiliation

der one another, and that we can now indulge in all manner of health destruction, neglect, and self-mediated abuse, should be all the evidence needed to realize that we have internalized hostility. Let us face up to what this means: nearly one hundred percent of our energy is required to process all the abuse in our lives, leaving us with little energy to compete in the white user-friendly American culture. It means that our grief is going to multiply. It means that, like hurting people who keep playing Russian roulette or cutting their wrists, we will continue to threaten suicide as we sink further into the deeper layers of trauma.

Internalized hostility

We routinely re-experience the trauma of psychic assault and spiritual abuse because the source of the pathology that has laid the foundation for our bouts of suicidal feelings is parasitically attached to our culture, and is both at home and in the black church. Black culture has thus become, on its surface, the mixture and sometimes the synthesis of the residues of our indigenous essence and relatively unseen grief-causing forces, which together have led to our shared patterns of belief, feeling, adaptation, definitions of reality, and guides of conduct in the American experience. Still, it is too much our grief that defines us as a people. Indeed, this is true to the degree that we can get together only in our grief.

Grief too much defines black peoplehood

At the same time, we ignore our grief in terms of processing it. Either by choice or some form of denial, the "keep silent" commandment helps the dis-ease thrive in the black church and community.

Need to confront grief

It is grief that hinders our wholeness and health, and it is our grief that we must confront! We must be confrontational in an effort to free our cultural practices from an addiction to unresolved grief as a basis for individual and group identity. And we must do the confronting aware of the fact that most of white America seems disinterested in our doing this for ourselves. Why the disinterest? Because once people are healed, they demand and will try to reclaim what is theirs, such as their indigenous heritage. This is the reason that, apart from the few whites who have spoken out, white America does not recognize that we are a grieving culture.

Jews supported in their griefwork

The Jews are recognized as a grieving culture, and prescriptions exist for how they are to be treated. Of course, this was not always true. The transmittable psychological injury was initially denigrated or denied, but the Jewish people never gave up. Now Jews are to be sympathetically supported as they work through their grief with Holocaust memorials and museums, as well as in their newly revitalized peoplehood, their undeterred pursuit of a homeland, their emigration to Israel, and their dual American-Israeli citizenship. We need the same tenacity and desire for respect and understanding. But we cannot even complete our grieving. We do not simply remain unrecognized as a grieving culture; we also have no indigenous place to call our home.

When we were still indigenous during slavery, we once made for the woods, dugouts, and swamps. Those were our places to go, in the manner of the American Indians who went off to their mountains and other sacred places. Now we say we go to church, but the church is a Western idea. Nor is the "black church" an indigenous place in the sense of village or community.

Importance of an indigenous place

Whenever we have tried to go back to Africa in the hope of finding our indigenous place, we have only brought our grief with us. This is one reason we have not been recognized as being home and sometimes have not found the reception that we imagined we should. The sense of insufferable loss is complicated when hardly anyone in Africa is crying for the return home of lost family members, or when no one from "home" comes looking for us. All of this just multiplies our grief as we learn that we are now indigenous to nowhere!

No one crying for our return

The worst part of all is that, even if we had an indigenous place to go, we still have not faced the reality of why we need such a place. Our souls are so abused, almost fatally injured, yet we do not even realize that we are wounded to the depths of our culture.

Lack of healthy identity

Part of our dilemma is our lack of a healthy sense of identity that produces outcomes beyond the emotional "feel-good" of entertaining worship services. The symptoms suggesting that we lack this healthy sense of identity are abundant in Sunday-morning mediocrity: prayers filled with religious fervor but empty of spiritual passion, preaching garnished with dramaturgy that portrays God as a scolding parent, artificial righteousness and ritualized claims of knowing God's mind, rote worship that fails to heal the brokenhearted, false barriers of purity and class distinction that separate believers from one another rather than binding them in spirit and community.

Black church rejection of spiritual edge

For too long, the black church has fashioned its services in a manner that rejects or undermines the prophetic and true spiritual edge of faith: entertaining gospel music but no emancipating gospel to confront the spiritual abuse that leaves us aimless and beholden to a narcissistic dominant overculture. Consequently, our need to be connected intimately to a God who is healthy has suffered to the degree that ecclesiastical purity is now largely a question of image, social justice is devalued, and structural injustice is justified by the strange notion of the inherent good—even righteousness—of economic status and privilege.

Some of us have rejected or undermined the prophetic and true spiritual edge of faith because we believe the victories of the affirmative action initiatives of the 1960s were sufficiently emancipative. As a black middle class emerged and was permitted to become a facsimile of the white middle class, we allowed our church doctrines to shift us further into a privileged, class-oriented dogma, in which some of our ministers now preach that the proper degree and correct form of faith will connect us to material gain.

Illusion of affirmative action successes

The result of this "get high quick" theology, similar to the effects brought about by cocaine use, has been that too many of us now believe God's favor shines upon those blessed to be conspicuous consumers. Then we turn around and cannot understand why the less privileged, who have felt little of the effects of the civil rights movement or affirmative action, often feel it too painful to attend church on a regular basis or at all. And churchfolk, in their disregard of outsiders, deafen their ears to the judgment ricocheting about the streets which says hardly any difference exists in the behavior of the churched and the unchurched, and the unchurched may even be the more honest.

Get high quick theology

I suggest that the Jesus worshiped on Sunday mornings offers us some degree of release, but that release

Sunday-morning Jesus

fails to provide us with durable solutions to our problems. Unlike the Jews, whom we have admired because of their refusal to let adversity overcome them, African Americans only follow up to a point the Jesus who died fighting. We love the Old Testament but have lost something in the transition from Judaism to black church.

Our problems have solutions and perhaps the Jesus who had neither house nor church in his homeland, offers real solutions. The conflict is that our preference for status and the status quo prevents our own indigenous religion—once a constant friend to our ancestors made hostages in an environment antagonistic to their nature—from "acting believing" that God meant to counteract the distorted and dysfunctional hegemonic forces of the chattel system. Our preference for status and the status quo keeps us bound to an imitation of white middle-class values and particularly to the notion of church as a place somewhere within the community. It might have been helpful at one time to speak of the "black church," in the sense of that autonomous black-owned property. But long before the terms black church and Negro church were coined by well-meaning scholars, village was all about a broader, more inclusive location.

While the abandoning of indigenous world views and practices, and the embracing of classical Western Chris-

Preference for status quo rather than the indigenous

tianity may have "worked" for those few who could successfully enroll in the American melting-pot experiment, these actions proved disastrous and even dangerous for African Americans in general. This religion of authority that supported a master-slave cultural paradigm produced a providence of God that lacked justice, required too much grace from the victims for unrepentant oppressors, denigrated the uniqueness of persons, mocked the omnipotence and goodness of God, and openly encouraged master-slave or sponsor-trustee relationships in the family of God.

American melting-pot experiment

The healing response we need is to be found in a spirituality that does not start or stop with Western Christian tradition and its emphasis on holy scripture, but rather in a spirituality rooted in core belief recorded in the history, hearts, and experiences of the people. The healing response is to be found in core belief handed down from one generation to the next, and in the overarching core belief that allows traditional beliefs to adjust to meet new circumstances in life, and thereby always remain realistic and pragmatic.

Spirituality rooted in indigenous core belief

We need a spirituality in which belief in the invisible world intersects with visible reality, so that faith is not an esoteric thing but a community function. We need a spirituality in which the spiritual and terrestrial life verify

Faith as a community function

each other in order for truth to be real, a spirituality in which healing the soul requires an attempt to determine what terrestrial-spiritual causes for symptoms and suffering are present. Ritual activities such as laying on of hands, anointing with oil, and prayer can be therapeutic; but, without an examination of the human or environmental sources of conflict and grief, we will continue to be plagued by a religious anesthesia that keeps us turning to short-term solutions that are best reserved for emergencies rather than for the long-term resolution of our problems.

Business as usual in the black church

Let us face it: with the way we tend to business in the black church, healing is rarely the sibling of maturity; the inductive and the experiential process of spirituality are hardly appreciated; and the religious focus is seldom on how all people are similar, what things they have in common, and how they cooperate, participate in collective responsibility, and value interdependence. Intuition is now counterfeited, creating superficial appreciations for symbolic imagery, inspiration, and revelation. Heartfelt, life-tested knowing is rarely the respected companion of knowledge gained through counting or measuring, the health of everyone's invisible spirit or essence is seldom based on a oneness with God and creation and on uplifting interpersonal relationships, and life becomes the exploitation of the division of opposites (either/or) rather than the discovery of ways to harmonize the union of seeming opposites (yin and yang).

We need a process of spiritual healing in which certain things are taking place: body and mind, relationships with others, society, and God are in harmony; undeveloped strengths, assets, and capacities are being accessed; persistent striving and evolving potentials are enhanced; the capacity to overcome fear of and resistance to growth is increased; good nutrition, exercise, and health are valued and sought, and people feel deserving of this; the intuitive/imaginative right-brain and rational/analytical left-brain capacities are integrated into a harmony (not separated by gender, for instance); life as opportunity is embraced, living in the present is possible, realistic hope for the future thrives and is energized; the ability to empathize with others is enhanced; the quality of close relationships and community caring increases (when we are spiritually healing, we care about the community we live in).

Process of spiritual healing

In the next chapter I will speak more along this line: soul therapy as one of the most healing functions of both the noninstitutional and the later institutional religious adaptations originating with Americans of African descent. These African Americans include indigenous

Healing function of soul therapy

preachers, pastors, conjurers, counselors, teachers, wise elders, griots, theologians, mothers, fathers, musicians, dancers, and artists who, living and promoting the indigenous art and science of God's providence, were intuitively aware that they were in the health business. These indigenous African Americans understood religion, culture, and human existence to be inseparable; they cared for core belief, ancient and adaptive, and described and prescribed health wherever needed and whenever possible; they made sure to create therapeutic places where black folk could eat, drink, dance, sing, play, and hear the counter-hegemonic stories that injected feelings of self-esteem and self-worth. Not all of them were Christian or "belonged to" a church; they simply understood the need for and accepted the responsibility of contributing to the "soul" of the black community.

The soul therapy I propose will have consequences similar to what I spoke of in my foreword: if one person starts to get free, the unfree are going to be upset, angry, and highly exposed. In other words, soul therapy is going to shatter the traditions and lies that have been spiritually abusive. Such therapy is not necessarily confrontational. It shatters unhealthy tradition simply by illuminating the indigenous ways by which people protect themselves from pain. It emphasizes and praises normal

Soul therapy shatters unhealthy tradition

responses to stress, celebrates the people's capacity for intimacy and reliance on relationship, shines a light on the dignified indigenous character, and passes on sacred core belief that celebrates the human essence of the people, defies the chattelization process, makes hope in eternal realities possible while facing daily impossibilities, and births joy in the adaptive, counter-aggressive, interrelated, highly therapeutic, psychologically-significant indigenous response-tradition of the African American experience.

In short, soul therapy involves cultivating attitudes about harmonious partnerships with Creator and creation; and it defines how information should be organized to promote health and wholeness, and to prevent, counteract, cope, and overcome insults. Combating the sin of spiritual abuse with passionate precision requires that the necessary resources be available in our personal/family bio-psycho-socio-spiritual health package and that those resources have as an objective the development of intuitively-affirmed ways of preventing psycho-spiritual pathology. This is what is meant by having "soul."

Having soul

A reconstructed and revitalized soul therapy insists on a psychology and theology of compassion that opposes a psychology and theology of control (competition, compulsion, and dualism). It encourages a psychology and theology of celebration (letting be, letting go, and letting dialectic happen). The quest for power, prestige, and possessions would then be seen for what it really is: an unfortunate symptomatic search for reassurance against anxiety. Power itself would be seen for what it is: an unfortunate brace against helplessness; prestige likewise an unfortunate buttress against humiliation; possessions an unfortunate prop against destitution. And the master-slave cultural paradigm, no matter how benevolent, would be seen for what it really is: an unfortunate form of "heaven" for only the few.

4

~ Soul Therapy ~

The positive view of creation among our indigenous black ancestors was rooted in a sensitivity to God's movement in the world: the birds flying, rivers roaring, flowers spreading their scent, yams sharing their nutrients, and human beings sharing their love. This external world affirmed what the inner-self understood, even from that initial merge of egg and sperm. Within the womb, as an attachment grew that was dependable and nurturing, and as the sense of touch, taste, and hearing emerged, each developing life listened to the rhythm of the mother's heartbeat and the contrapuntal beating of her or his own heart amid the whooshing sounds of embryonic fluid and the assorted audible expressions of the mother's gastrointestinal tract and respiratory system. Muted but definite voices emanated from the world outside the womb, that first biological Garden of Eden. The most reassuring sound from that outside world was the mother's voice, accompanied by the sensations of rushing blood, adrenaline surges, near weightlessness, the freedom of swimming, the taste of embryonic fluid, and caresses. Then

Positive view of creation

came rhythmic contractions, the pressure of the push through the vaginal canal, the release of birth, the rush of inspiration, the reconnection felt in bonding, the warmth and sustenance of the mother's milk, and the cheers of the family. Deep within the subconscious of each human life, the biological and psychological origins of soul therapy are planted!

Objective of soul therapy

Turning now from the womb experience to the harshness of reality, we find the objective of soul therapy illustrated in the movie *Rosewood* (a story derived from real life). The heroic black man in the movie, Mr. Mann, hangs by the neck from a rope for the second time in his forty years, surrounded by people who do not "care enough" that he is innocent or that they are lynching a Medal of Honor World War I veteran. "A nigger is a nigger," one white father evangelizes, naturally wanting the best for his son: wanting him to grow up "righteous" in a manner special to their race alone. "God made things the way they are," the father promises the son. Even the emaciated attempt of the white woman, who claimed a "nigger" beat her in order to hide an affair with a white convict gone awry, cannot be heard over the din of the white community's core belief: a nigger is a nigger. "The nigger refuses to die," the crowd says with camouflaged respect. "He'll die, even though he didn't do anything," the ranking law enforcement official eulogizes. Mr. Mann's only crime was being a black man who wanted peace with dignity in this land to which his ancestors came in chains and into which he was born in pain.

Intent on choosing the time and place of his own death, Mr. Mann takes control of the only thing left him. Against the wishes of the culture's masters, Mr. Mann willfully resists strangulation, frees his hands, pulls up the weight of his body with one hand while fetching a small utility knife from his boots with the other, and cuts himself free. He runs to his horse, grabs the saddle, commands the horse to go, and is dragged away to freedom.

Inside Mr. Mann is the initial environmental experience of the womb, those pre-intrauterine (with God) and intrauterine experiences of safety, security, and stability. These invisible-spiritual and visible-biological bases offer an understanding of the ancestor's indigenous celebrations of creation, whole-self communion, transcendence, and overall connection with the world and its maker, the alpha and omega. This indigenousness that Mr. Mann inherited is the spiritual context of soul therapy, as it seeks to organize health information in a manner that will help people prevent, counteract, cope with, and overcome the insults to their humanity. It is indigenous-

Overcoming insult to inner humanity

ness that does not permit one to define self based on someone else's illusions!

In a life replete with trauma and grief, Mr. Mann must have made use of the available therapeutic interventions of "soul," both to prevent injury to and to heal his mind, body, and spirit. Such prevention and healing are especially important because of the utter destructiveness of domino trauma, in which trauma after trauma collide on a daily basis, especially in the middle of a dominant culture that is unable or refuses to validate as healthy any reaction black people have to trauma.

Therapeutic intervention of soul

In practical terms, Mr. Mann survived the lynching because he had healthy self-esteem, that crucial element that forms the basis of any appreciation or use of indigenousness. How do we know that Mr. Mann had healthy self-esteem? We perceived it in his confidence, in his ability to be rational in a traumatic situation, and in his readiness to overcome yet another challenge in life. We also know it because Mr. Mann simply understood that he had the right to assert his needs and wants, to achieve his values, to enjoy the fruits of his efforts, and to be alive. High self-esteem of Mr. Mann's kind turns mere life into a liveliness that seeks challenges by establishing meaningful and demanding goals, provides energy for coping with and overcoming problems, fuels the ambi-

Healthy self-esteem and self-image

tion to realize full potential, expresses inner riches, supports openness and honesty, attracts one to nourishing instead of toxic relationships, and takes the chip off one's shoulder because people and their opinions are no longer fatally threatening.

A man or woman without healthy self-esteem, a "good nigger" type, would have accepted execution at the hands of the people who do not "care enough," convinced that these "righteous" people would not lie, could not make mistakes, and did not possess evil intentions. Such a type feels safe enough with whites to discard the indigenous heritage and to trade in the indigenous idea of the "collective I" for the "individual I," or even the disposition of the "I got mine, too bad you don't have yours." A "good nigger" type internalizes his or her victimization, even revels in it, and thereby short-circuits any transformative power that might allow for some coming to grips with abuse and trauma—or coming to grips with any loss while yet being able to appreciate what is left. For the "good nigger," the path of determining life's meaning becomes a dead end road, and the ability to shift from feelings of limitations to thoughts of possibilities dies. We witness this demise in the Rosewood black community, where all the preaching, singing, prophesizing,

Good nigger type

and praying for divine intervention results in no helpful hand against the white terror.

In the abundant faith in the "Jesus" of those ritual acts of churchly catharsis, a Jesus who is removed from his radical roots in Judaism, we have what I call the Rosewood phenomenon. This is the phenomenon of a "Jesus" who does not save lives. The matriarch of the small black town, who believed her blue-eyed Jesus "saves" and yet knew "how white people could be," was shot in the stomach on her front porch while reminding the whites of her longtime service and intimate relationship with most of them. The black pastor was shot in the heart, his wife hung, and his church burned. And the church bell was rung to celebrate this ritual of white supremacy. It was in fact sacred ritual which symbolizes the fact that black churchly catharsis has a time and place in the healing and growth process but is not and must not be an end in itself, particularly in master-slave contexts.

In contrast to what was evidenced in the Rosewood community, African American religion originally served as mediator between black people and the dominant culture. Our indigenous religious community of soul therapists assisted us to develop a resilient self-concept which could fend off the lethal intrusions of the master culture. This sort of "church" was an extended family or group

Jesus who does not save

Indigenous black religion

of extended-family networks with therapeutic value and potential, whose goal of spiritual maturity and emotional health was implemented by verifying an understanding of God (collective lessons of life validated by experience and passed on in both sacred and secular forms) within the context of family and community relationships.

What of this "Rosewood phenomenon" then? How comes it? It comes into being when lies are preferred over truth. Lies can meet certain culturally mandated psycho-socio-spiritual needs, like the need to hide feelings of low self-esteem, shame, and other symptoms of dis-ease, such as guilt. Lies can hide these feelings only temporarily, however, for there will come a day when severe consequences erupt and control is lost.

Lies preferred over truth

One such lie preferred over truth is that churchfolk are trustworthy. The indigenous among our enslaved forebears, sensitive to the psychological effects of chattelization, never took for granted that all slaves could be trusted. For reasons of psychological health there is a need to trust and a need for trust, but those early protectors of soul routinely held these opposites in tension, constantly shifting as needed between the polarities. Therefore, while in the white world a Mr. Mann could trust neither whites (even in their most benevolent demonstrations) nor blacks (even those who were church-

Trust and soul therapy

goers), the nucleus of soul therapy was based on fully trusting in the providence of God. The solution to the "Rosewood phenomenon," then, requires that truth not be left unspoken, but that it be confronted and the revealed sources of injustice be dealt with and eliminated and adequate restitution for any victims be settled.

Wasteful grace

When confronted in this manner, one truth is that grace is wasted on people who do not "care enough"; that attempts to save such people, at the expense of one's own health and safety, is a waste of heartbeats and breaths. Another truth is that, no matter how sincere we have been in trying to be "faithful" (like the Rosewood pastor and matriarch), kill-the-nigger fever can strike at any time among whites. We can either accept this fate, meekly knowing "how white folk can be"; or we can do as Mr. Mann did: participate in the divine providence by having an effective contingency plan. This chapter is about that plan, which I call soul therapy.

Racism meets psychological needs

Soul therapy necessitates that we speak plainly about the effects of racism on the perpetrators who benefit from the racist behavior and system, including how such racism meets certain psychological needs in those who embrace power and privilege. But while the ideal of soul therapy is that white folks be "saved," or treated and cured of their problem, soul therapy is more immediately concerned in helping black folks get liberated in the midst of the spiritual abuse that not only victimizes us but makes us our own victimizers.

Allow me to enter this discussion of soul therapy by saying more about truth, a concept on which soul therapy firmly stands; and specifically by recollecting August 28, 1963, the day Martin Luther King, Jr. spoke at the Lincoln Memorial for the March on Washington. I was there with my father, a nationally recognized civil rights leader, one of the thousands sympathetic to what Dr. King was calling a Dream; and I heard Dr. King say that we had come there to dramatize a shameful condition and to cash a check promised by the Declaration of Independence and the Constitution, a check that was supposed to give us opportunities provided by "the riches of freedom and the security of justice." America had defaulted on this promissory note, Dr. King claimed, for the Negro's check had come back marked "insufficient funds."

Truth and soul therapy

A few years earlier, on June 6, 1961, in his "The American Dream" speech at Lincoln University, in Pennsylvania, Dr. King gave a hint as to how severe the American condition was and how long it had persisted: "Ever since the Founding Fathers of our nation dreamed this noble Dream, America has been something of a schizophrenic personality, tragically divided against herself. On the one hand we proudly professed the principles of democracy, and on the other hand we have sadly the very antithesis of those principles." So, what is the truth? The truth is, this "condition"—our unrequited American Dream—remains the perennial African American condition.

Why truth is suppressed

To understand why, let us just ask ourselves what would happen if America chose to permit us the realization of the Dream? It would be necessary for Americans to admit that dysfunctional relationships, psychological addiction, and co-dependency have been interwoven into our national culture and that all Americans have lost health and life at the hands of a disease that is insidious, progressive, contagious, and fatal (in the Rosewood sense). It would be necessary for Americans to stop reshaping Christian theologies to justify cultural narcissism; we would have to take our common denial off the honor roll and inform our leaders that we are tired of a schizophrenic Dream that tragically divides us against ourselves.

It would be necessary to allow all voices that make up America to have a place in articulating the meaning of the Dream. It would be necessary to dismantle structures and ideologies that perniciously and violently control the social order, including systemic church-as-usual ideologies. It would be necessary to teach American children how hypocritical it was for the Founding Fathers to write documents containing language such as "we the people" while knowingly not including all of the people. It would be necessary to dethrone the generational effects of racism on all shades of Americans and to offer educations that require a new ethic of inclusiveness on the part of administrators, teachers, students, and parents. It would be necessary to restructure our economic world view and put people over profits and help people become producers instead of consumers. And until all this takes place, it would be necessary to recognize anger as a sign of health in those people who remain unfairly excluded from the Dream.

These requisites comprise a tall order, which explains why the unrequited American Dream remains the perennial national condition of African Americans. Yet, only with the realization of the foregoing requisites will the children of former slaves and slaveowners ever be able to sit down to a table of brotherhood and sisterhood, states from Mississippi to Minnesota ever become oases of freedom and justice, and the content of human character ever be permitted to outweigh the importance of race. Here alone lies the means by which the rough places may be made plain, the crooked places

The requisites of justice

made straight, and the glory of the Lord revealed on all flesh!

A certain scripture says that those who say I love God and yet hate their brothers and sisters are liars, for people who do not love those whom they have seen cannot love God whom they have not seen. Every time I see this particular verse, it tells me that Americans do not have much choice if we are going to be people of God. So unless we are going to throw out our biblical belief, we must examine ourselves as to whether we are liars or lovers. If we are going to be liars, people who merely say with meager words that we love God, then we will continue in any theology, any psychology, or any economic program that is in actuality unloving. But if we are going to be people who are not liars, then we are given a commandment that we must love both God and one another.

All who wish to be God-loving bearers of truth, including African Americans, must first admit to another precept that is a foundational part of the validity of soul therapy: good people and good things have come out of Africa. How do we know? Because some of our most persevering, life-sustaining core beliefs came with the people shipped in chains to America. Is it not because of the goodness and effectiveness of those indigenous core

Liars or lovers

Good things out of Africa

SOUL THERAPY

beliefs that the science of chattelization had to be elevated to an art form in order for slavery to work? The effectiveness of soul therapy is dependent on the nature and quality of our core beliefs, those bedrock attitudes in charge of our deliberate behavior, relationships, and spontaneous responses to crisis and blessing. These are beliefs which, taken together, indicate whether we have faith that God can be trusted.

We can raise the question about the nature and quality of our core beliefs because they are not completely innate characteristics. Core beliefs are acquired through culture and developed out of life experience, which means that these beliefs can also be distorted, diminished, and destroyed. In fact, know how to create some sick folk? Distort, diminish, or destroy their faith and make sure they cannot trust! Make sure their core beliefs are so screwed up that, anytime they are blessed, their psychological response is self-destructive! Want to do something to others that they understand to be against God's will and want them to participate in the sense of the "Rosewood phenomenon"? Affect how those folk think about or trust God!

Source and importance of core beliefs

On the other hand, the element unique to our enslaved indigenous ancestors and those folk similar to Mr. Mann, who maintained their indigenousness against all odds, is that they were doing something that psychologically allowed them to sustain their foundational trust in the Creator. This is what soul therapy must do for us today: be a means of overcoming, not merely coping. Jesus did not say I came into the world to cope with it. I think he said somewhere that he had come to overcome it!

Overcoming rather than mere coping

We seek our health and wholeness. Perhaps we can best envision this objective as the classic dialectical tension between good and evil, in which evil is conceived of as good that has been distorted. Were we to remove the distortion we would be left with the good. In the same manner, since the creation of human life was considered good, the original plans must have been that we should be healthy; and if we were intended to be healthy, then whatever we were intended to believe ought to lead us to that health.

Healthiness in the original plans

This question of what is psychologically right in people is at the extreme opposite of the question of what is psychologically wrong with people (pathology), which has been a specialty in Western science. Although history and we ourselves have depicted the Africans enslaved in America as some very weak people, the way our indigenous forebears dealt with their needs, surviving and thriving on certain core beliefs, testifies to how they were able to relinquish those aspects of living that were of lesser value than their highest needs—spiritual well-being and sustenance.

Prioritizing of spiritual well-being

If today we are having a problem surviving, then perhaps we need to follow suit in placing life's priorities: we may have to relinquish our territory in order to save our ability to think, or relinquish our safety needs in order to keep our identity. We are always trying to save our souls, in other words, because even if our minds and bodies are intact, they are of no consequence if our souls, once under attack, fall down wounded and die.

So, when the master tried to develop a culture among slaves and their descendants that promoted addiction to the Anglo-Saxon culture by means of co-dependant relationships—an effort that required him to distort our view of self, God, and the world in order to turn what was powerful within our group into a weakness—a lot of the enslaved said *no*, and a lot of them were killed as a consequence. And some of the enslaved said they would just pretend to go along with the master's intentions. For those who just pretended and for those who said no and yet remained alive, it was soul therapy, rooted in a certain set of core beliefs, that sustained them.

Refusal to compromise higher values

The rest of the slaves who said *yes* to co-dependent relationships with the master culture were trained to an-

Compromise of higher values

ticipate the needs of and feel responsible for the master, seek the approval and the attention of the master, and feel anxious and guilty when the master had a problem. We still see that today! What else? The "yes" slaves were trained to do things to please the master even when they did not want to, to depend on the master to define their wants and needs, to believe that the master knew what was best for them without their input, to focus all their energy on the master and his happiness, to fear being away from the master and on their own, to believe the master no matter what his behavior or whether it was trustworthy, and to show no anger when denied what they needed. We still think that way! In fact, one of the master's tests of good slaves is to deny their needs and see if they get angry, like denying them the right to bring their cultural inputs into the workplace, permitting them to express their culture only down in the slave quarters.

More compromise

What else? The slaves who did not say *no* to co-dependency with the master culture were taught to be happy when feeling unappreciated, to blame other slaves or themselves when things went wrong, to have heart-stopping fear of making mistakes, to do anything to be more liked or loved by the master, to let others hurt them or their kindred without trying to offer protection, to pretend that bad things were not happening when they were. We are still like that today! And what is the yes-slave to do? Just keep working. And do not stop, because then you might start thinking some white thoughts—like, "vacation"!

How else were those yes-slaves to behave? Find it difficult to empathize for and feel close to other slaves. (Is it any wonder that today we are having problems with relationships?) Feel that they are behaving like "niggers" when trying to be spontaneous or have fun. (We have churches that try to leave our indigenous spontaneity behind because of the negative images their co-dependency has taught them to attach to these practices.) Fear abandonment to the point that they feel it necessary to put up with almost anything; then feel that they have to coerce, manipulate, beg, or bribe to get what they want. Feel helpless and powerless to change themselves or their situation. Treat members of their own group worse than they treat people outside the group, using such behaviors as pretense and false flattery, which cheapen human dignity in the interest of mere self-sustenance. Hide true feelings behind a facade of passive acquiescence, sometimes to the point of fantasy. We even have fantasy religions today: symbolic status striving, pomp and circumstance, showmanship, and ritual incantations we presume to have healing power.

Still more compromise

We see what was done psychologically to make human beings from Africa accept the condition of enslavement. What was done extends to include those factors that today make us act as if none of this was done and as if none of this continues to be done. We do not even believe that our minds have been tampered with or that this tampering has affected our theology, church, and our understanding of spirituality.

Good trustees of the system

What was done continues to be done! What the dominant group hates, today's yes-slaves, the good trustees of the system, are ashamed of to the point of self-hate and denial of their indigenous heritage. Even worse, these co-dependent trustees are the ones who raise cane about certain folks in the community being too militant, rather than recognizing these indigenous soul-bearers as rightfully and healthfully countering the aggression that regularly bombards them. Even as the yes-slaves speak of fighting against the spiritual "powers and principalities," they yet perceive militancy as a problem that must be quelled in the church. Notice how the psyche allows people to separate those two concepts—spiritual abuse and its militant counter-attack—so that we are incapable of seeing any relationship between the two! What this means is that Rosewood folk will shout "Jesus, Jesus, Jesus," and the result may be very cathartic and help them cope with the moment; but when those folk walk back outside that church building, nothing will help them deal with the Legion they are bound to confront.

This is not at all to suggest that black worship does not offer us a healing balm. Good black preaching, for instance, helps set the stage for healing. Emotion-laden problems can be reframed in seemingly spontaneous ways. Emotional arousal can move one to catharsis, and a congregation can begin to cry, shout, and join the rhythmic flow (breathing based) of the sermon. Traumatic memories can be uncovered and released. And in all this, music increases the cathartic potential. Such rituals may help worshipers access inner resources for creative solutions, whose achievement can be heard in the language of a people's culture or world view: "I've been to the mountaintop," "Ah ha," "The Spirit spoke to me," "It came to me," "I was suddenly free," "It was a miracle," "I woke up with the answer," "Prayer changes things."

Healing process in black worship

There really ought to be something deeply therapeutic and lasting every time black folk go to church, something that addresses not simply the surface of the hurt but the deepest degrees of grief down in the creases of our souls, something that will give the soul a healing balm even before the beatings and the murder rain down. But what we have far too often (imagine this, because it

Reality of abuses in black church

is occurring all over the country) are pastors who receive grief-stricken congregants into their offices for private counseling and then proceed to apply a balm of a different sort, having seduced the confidant who is vulnerable. Or they allow themselves to give in to seductions coming from people who are co-dependent and wish to drain the minister of what they perceive to be balmy, holy juices. And some of these pastors do not see or admit to any conflict between this kind of behavior and the call to preach the word of God! They are perpetrators, and they have both victims and witnesses enthralled right in their churches.

Paradigm of perpetration

Let us talk again about perpetrators, starting once more with the slavemaster, who is the paradigmatic model. And let us keep in mind that the hardest abuse to heal is the kind that leaves no open wound, visible scar tissue, or bruises; and that the invisible but real abuse is usually the most damaging form of trauma a person or a people can experience. The fact is, too, that in such cases the perpetrator can more easily deny any attack, the victim can find such attack harder to prove, and the witness can justify doing nothing because of the lack of firm evidence.

Say we have a master who, after putting his white wife to bed at night in a room all by herself (because she is untouchable except for procreation thus saith the Lord), goes down the hill and engages in all kinds of perverse sexual acts with his female slaves, perhaps even in front of their children (or maybe their husbands); or even "in front of" their unborn children, insofar as the physical apparatus necessary for personality development is so fragile that even the unborn child of a pregnant slave could be affected by the mother's terror as her unresolved flight response causes the intrauterine experience to become biochemically hostile. So here is the slavemaster's son, Billy, a witness growing up around all of this. And one day Billy says, "Daddy, where do you go every night?" "Son, when you become a man I'll take you down the hill and show you." When Billy eventually gets down the hill, he asks, "Is this the way men act?" "Yes." "Oh!" So after that first generation, the behavior becomes part of the culture; which is why the witness is potentially the most dangerous person in an abusive system, even more dangerous than perpetrator or victim. Once the abuse gets put into place with a little power and a little purpose, all that is required is to show the behavior to those who are up and coming in privilege, and they will say, "Hey, this is not a bad deal; I can have one woman up at the big house and all of these women down here in the quarters." If certain people

Perpetration becomes tradition

have been used to going down the hill and raping other people, it is a habit now. Been doing it for years! Dad did it! Grandpa did it! So the sons and their sons find creative ways to do it too, even though slavery has been over now for years.

Difficulty of breaking tradition

Dysfunctional relationships, psychological addictions, and co-dependancy have thus become parasitically interwoven into the general American culture, making normal the tendency of people to believe that it is not only profitable but acceptable for one group of people to do these kinds of perverse things to another group of people. And once such normality sets in, no one can see the problem anymore! This means that the people who have benefitted from the perpetration are sick to the point of not knowing it.

Some people do know it, or have discovered it. And how cruel and abusive it is when the white preachers who know or discover these things just go on preaching a pack of lies. Then again, what a terrible experience it would be for white folks to be awakened by their preachers telling them that their present reality was set up by their forebears to permit them simply to inherit power and privilege at the violent expense of all other humanity.

Can we imagine what might happen to a white pastor who discovers the truth that not only was Jesus not white, but he did not act white: he did not agree to treat every Roman as his superior, did not accept the idea that love should never be expected to be the love of equals in matters concerning Romans and his own people of color, did not accept the idea that he could never assert or intimate that a Roman might by lying or demonstrating dishonorable intentions, did not accept the idea that he could never lay claim to or overtly demonstrate superior spirituality or intelligence to the Romans, did not give up his ministry because the penalties for not following proper political etiquette were severe or warranting of a cruel Roman death? Can we imagine that white minister, who by now has been labeled a "nigger lover," then saying to his congregation: "My brothers and sisters, we're going to have to move from the suburbs back into the city, because the Lord we have been worshiping looks more like those folk we left behind than like us out here; and because we're just plain hypocrites if we keep moving further and further out." White folks have been damaged by the racism and slavery they have witnessed!

Jesus not white

Black folks have been damaged too, which is my point. Our perpetrations run parallel to the white paradigm, and they create similar victims and witnesses among our own. Yet how can these things be happening to us if we are good church folk? These things can be happen-

Perpetration in the black tradition

ing in church if soul therapy is not happening; for if we so much as distort or devalue the intent of soul therapy, the process becomes an opiate that reduces people to dependent, developmentally-paralyzed, psychologically-sterile walking zombies.

Countering tradition of soul therapy

Once again, soul therapy must have sprung from the initial environmental experience of safety, security, and stability, perhaps concurrent with attempts to prevent the fears and anxieties associated with daily existence. As human beings began to move beyond the mere sensory observation of environmental order, they doubtless sought on the spiritual level to celebrate and communicate their souls' relationship with the world and its Creator. The soul therapy that evolved from this was fashioned into something dynamic and holistic and had as one of its gifts the discovery, development, and use of intuitively experienced and affirmed ways of being that prevented psycho-spiritual pathology.

Brought to America within the hearts of African slaves, soul therapy involved our harmonious partnerships with Creator and creation for the purpose of a health and wholeness that would enable us to prevent, counteract, cope, and overcome insults to who we were; to find ways to neutralize and remove dissonance from the interplay of mind, body, spirit, and environment; and to achieve our

God-given potential. Soul therapy provided a guide for the construction of relationship-based infrastructures that established within us hope, self-determination, a sense of purpose, a sense of competence, a sense of self, a sense of how to belong, a healthy perspective on love, and an appreciation for learning and wisdom. By countering pressures that could crush identity, soul therapy mediated the struggle for sanity in insane situations.

Soul therapy mediates oppression

So the African American indigenous response to the New World experience originally served as a clear mediator between our people and what society said about us and did to us. Today, however, the black church at best embraces but a residue of that response. Even the use of music in our churches is but a remnant of what it once was for indigenous forebears always reconnecting to a Creator moving with and within creation: altered states of consciousness brought on by the interplay of rhythms, tones, textures, silences, and movements prevented pathology and promoted healing and harmony while helping to engender the holistic aims of the providential God. The oral tradition, consisting of stories, proverbs, and folktales, was a proven tradition for connecting a person to a liberating past. There was history-sharing, talking, praying, correcting, analysis of problems, reality checks, times for expression, medicinal food and drink, abreac-

Only a residue of soul therapy

tion, conscious-altering music, dance, song, catharsis, relaxation, re-interpretation, re-education and re-enforcement, support offerings, identity and relationship-building—all formed around time-tested core beliefs. The resulting inner dialogues that these genres engendered were strengthened in the crucible of daily struggle.

Therapy of secular music

Yet today we see a breakdown of soul therapy, a failure that usually has its genesis in the prisms of personality differences, imbalanced and unhealthy distrust, and the mixed theological messages that went into African American religious adaptations. The failure has been such that we are now uncertain as to whether soul music is capable of activating soul healing via the re-enforcement of healthy core beliefs; whether blues, jazz, and rhythm and blues are as capable as gospel in removing obstacles from the mind/body's natural tendency to self-heal.

Music can therapeutically rebuild

The activation of self-healing in the soul is helped by music, especially when music is synergistically connected to movement. The music that makes us feel best, as it rebuilds our requisite core beliefs amid fatiguing battles, can be stored up to ready us for upcoming bouts; and dance, with its persistent power and positiveness, can bring forth this "memory," even amidst our most traumatic states of mind. The key for the therapy-oriented music minister, in collaboration with the pastor, is

SOUL THERAPY

selecting music that goes beyond conscious logic, freeing up the trauma response so that the beneficial recollections can be tapped. This process is not unlike what happens when healthy restorative feelings come from listening to music we loved as children, where healthy breakthroughs give us the feeling of, say, wanting to thank our parents or other family members for loving us when we were youthful and vulnerable.

When I first came to understand how utterly important are the synergistic connections of music and movement to healthy core belief, I was yet an undergraduate in the late 1960s. I was attending a Christian liberal arts college in the Midwest which was attempting to stay in step with the civil rights movement by bringing in the largest number of African American freshmen in the school's history, all athletes. Not only were we a grossly outnumbered "minority," a grand total of twenty-seven of us out of nearly two thousand students, but the college was unprepared to meet our social needs due to the racial insensitivity of many of the white faculty, staff, and students.

Initial discovery of soul therapy

One of the football coaches, who offered the incentives of "soul food" to help us play better, recommended that we do our "real socializing" off-campus. Because one of the new recruits had been seen by a coach's wife as being "too friendly" with a white coed, he was even told where (in a larger town nearby) he could find "colored girls" for "social purposes." This coach's talk with the recruit took place beside the football status chart, on which the student noticed that he had just fallen from second to fourth string. Another football player received a serious brain concussion while making a tackle, and the locker room was full of discussion during that week about how much a "colored boy" could actually suffer from a concussion.

Personal experience of racism

Not only was it disheartening that racism was thriving unobstructed at an institution of higher learning, but this was a Christian college where the love ethic (not the Jim Crow ethic) was supposed to be operative in determining a student's significance. The Christian idealism that permeated the campus seemed promising, but daily experiences informed us that our value did not exceed our identity as a cargo of dark-hued gladiators recruited to help the all-white school win in collegiate sports. We were subsisting in a deceptively camouflaged Jim-Crow infrastructure that voraciously devoured the reserves in our belief systems!

Need for soul ministry

Not long after our arrival at the college campus, therefore, we found ourselves needing a soul ministry that would bring us relief from living within a Eurocentric dichotomous reality. We needed grace treatments in order to remain free of a tempting neurotic dependency on the approval or acceptance of the white majority. So, we coveted a place where we could "turn up the volume" and submerge ourselves in the musical sounds that might help empower our souls to counter the endless corrosion of our well-being. We sought grace treatments that would come from the sounds of black music and would permit us to carve out a psychic space where we could take deep breaths, submerge ourselves in the spirit, and then emerge from within the interstices of our victimization to become co-protectors of one another—co-soul therapists.

We began a midweek meeting in the dorm room of one of our brothers, mobilized our collective heritage of "soul," and out of the sustained racial hostility and injustice at the college emerged a shared experience of power and perseverance. There, the first liberating testimony came from the song "Old Man River" on the album *Temptations Live!* As we listened to the soul-healing music, our indigenous ancestors began speaking to us through the wisdom of Old Man River, one who always manages to prevent his soul from becoming psycho-spiritually anemic in this hostile world. The wisdom told us that tough times would pass, and everything would

Mobilizing collective heritage of soul

be all right, and that our seemingly impossible task was to keep "rollin' along."

Affirmations of song

We danced and sang our agreement with what the Temptations seemed to understand about our personal and collective deprivations in this hostile white environment: "Old Man River don't say nothin', must know somethin', just keeps rollin' along." This was in fact our reality! If we were going to endure through our emancipation proclamation of graduation and reap the payoff of a door-opening education, we could say absolutely nothing around whites of what we were really feeling or thinking.

The Temptations' album had a kind of sermonic build-up; and in the final song, "Don't Look Back," the singers seemed to know the one ingredient essential for their exhortations to be cemented within us. With deep hunger we seized upon their words: "Just put your hand in my hand, walk and don't look back." Together, hand-in-hand, we told one another that we could make it, that none of us had to try to make it alone. We said encouraging words like the Temptations: "I know you've been hurt by someone else...I've been hurt too; I know just what to do." Without the sealant of love, our push toward psychological health and liberation would not have lasted; but by affirming the principle of knowing just how much we could bear, we reaffirmed the core belief we had always heard in church: that someone larger and more powerful than everyone knows just how much we can bear.

The Legion who victimized us at the college viewed our expressions of release as evidence of childlike or primitive intellects. Their affront—"Turn down that jungle music!"—came through our dormitory door like a well-tested cruise missile and was but another interruption that reminded us of our "place." We did turn down our music; and with that one incremental twist of the volume, we were overwhelmed by cacophony that penetrated our soul's oasis from the adjacent rooms—the Beach Boys, the Monkees, and the Beatles. This was music being used to combat the loneliness, depression, and homesickness of the white students, but it reminded us again of the pernicious double-standard that caused our subsistence at the school to be torturous and traumatic.

Lacking outside appreciation

As I began to make sense of our unarticulated means of survival in that hostile environment, I mused over our use of music as therapy and even discussed my ideas in psychology class. One of my professors informed me that the use of music I had described was typical of a people with limited analytical abilities, but there was re-

Early discussion of soul therapy potential

ally nothing of authentic therapeutic value in black music. This response only pushed me to think that the traditional therapy offered by whites—people like my psychology professor to whom our music was noise—could not be entirely healthy for us; that acceptance of and proper respect for the cultural strengths of a people must be mandatory for a professional to enter into healing relationships with members of that group. I was also pushed to think further about how far a "soul" therapy could go in helping our people overcome certain psychological obstacles. After all, our indigenous forebears enslaved in America did not have access to professional therapy; yet their music helped them overcome the most abject oppression and trauma.

Wellsprings of power

Over time it became increasingly evident to me that black culture was informed and infused by musical sounds and meanings replete with wellsprings of power. The evidence was obvious: no other people in history so severed from their homelands and indigenous ways of life and so abjectly oppressed, as the Africans enslaved in America, had come through slavery having created such an immense body of soul-mending music. Thinking about this, in light of the therapeutic use of music by my college friends and me, the idea of building a professional, music-based therapy came to me. In fact, it now seemed only too obvious: people bring to any helping relationship a system of core belief that aids them in their survival, and our music can plant, cultivate, and support those beliefs of the soul. The strategic emphasis of a therapy that built on this tradition would therefore hinge on effectively eliciting and/or planting healthy core beliefs in the intuitive and the emotive sectors of consciousness with the help of a prescribed musical diet.

At best our music serves our soul therapy tradition of adaptive, counter-aggressive, interrelated, highly therapeutic, and psychologically significant religious response to our troubled experience in the world. Our religion is at its best when it represents our capacity to balance ourselves, to be healthy and prosperous, and to "make it through" even as our hearts and minds are under attack. In this regard, the black church should comprise one extended "rite of passage" that takes our people from the opportunities and responsibilities of childhood to the opportunities and responsibilities of adulthood, so that we are able to realize our fullest potential and become contributing members of our communities.

Black church as rite of passage

We generally understand "rites of passage" to function in the capacity of passing along core beliefs, character requirements, life-skills—in general, the culture necessary for individual citizens or villagers to find their adult

Rites of passage defined

place within a society. Perhaps most importantly, then, rites of passage involve the transfer of essential values. Justice is one important value especially relevant today. It involves honoring the dignity of each human being, regardless of any specific attributes—race, gender, economic status, intellectual endowment, or physical prowess—which might differentiate people and possibly prevent someone from having the same considerations, privileges, and love.

Rites of passage should not only connect individuals to spiritual and mental growth, but also to physical growth and to goals that include everyday activities. In offering definitions of what people really need to accomplish, rites of passage should have timetables for completion and guidelines for the conditions under which such timetables may be extended and the deadlines reset. Progress should be measurable, and thus the expectations for the passage must be clear.

Ideal of black church passage

If the black church functions as a "rite of passage" within the larger black community, the process of the "passage" includes the following ideals, to name a few: 1) the grasping of an understanding and appreciation of the old self, 2) a casting off of the old self and the development of a vision of a future self, 3) the identification, acknowledgment, and appreciation of the new self, 4) the recognition and celebration of the consequential growth with family and community, 5) the demonstration of gratitude to everyone involved in the passage.

Church members should then be able to define and demonstrate a sense of spiritual health as it relates to self, others, and human systems; define, understand, and demonstrate the responsibilities of spiritual adulthood; and demonstrate and explain healthy core beliefs consistent with the responsibilities of spiritual adulthood. Such responsibilities include the ability to form bonds with others who are healthy in the context of our complex history of psycho-social development; the ability to work in any role necessary, as leader or follower, without feeling arrogant or devalued, toward the goal of contributing to an uplifting and supportive environment for all; the ability to explain puberty, maturation, and right attitudes toward the role of sex in life; the ability to take care of the body and work toward physical potential, and thus understand the interconnection of body and mind; and the ability to explain and demonstrate the healing role of the soul therapist and articulate a vision of a community in which everyone is a responsible and healthy participant.

Soul therapists who attain "passage" will possess traits of availability, reliability, respectability, incorruptibility, empathy, consistency, dedication, and faithfulness in the

Soul therapists who attain passage

growth of their people. They will understand and help the community practice beliefs and strategies designed to counteract all forms of injury, recognize the wide variety of reactions and responses to trauma with the community, and understand that problems of survival can be met by relinquishing a lesser need and emphasizing the restorative functions of healthy core belief. In other words, "passaged" soul therapists—not only emancipated, but liberated—will honor the experience their people have while seeking to "make sense" of their own experience.

5

~ *Conclusion* ~

We spend most of our lives working in earnest to acquire things that make life worthwhile. We crave friends, a spouse, children, employment, a home, security, and a future. We expect to be hurt by occasional loss, but we do not expect such loss to become chronic, soul-fragmenting, and seemingly eternal. While all people suffer loss and trauma at one time or another, African Americans can face high degrees of traumatic loss because of their unique possibility to feel blue as they suffer from being black. Our reactions to this blue-black trauma have sometimes turned into post-traumatic pathologies when they have been interpreted through a cultural lens that is unconnected with their history or genesis. But by orienting ourselves within our community, we can move systematically to prevent such reaction to trauma from invading other healthier bio-psycho-socio-spiritual domains.

Feeling blue and being black

Soul therapy makes available the necessary resources in the bio-psycho-socio-spiritual health package of individuals, families, and communities. It depends on people who understand what our souls are lacking, especially in the hands of our oppressors, and what theological forms our soul support needs. Soul therapists are people who understand how essential it is to validate the normalcy of our response to trauma. They also make sense out of the nonsense of nonresponse or dissociation as a coping mechanism.

It was against the chattelization process that traumatized blacks as it sought to mold them into good slaves (and even better ex-slaves) that black religion once stood in the tradition of soul therapy. But the black church now fails to take an adequate stand against this same phenomenon of chattelization. We say in the church that God is in us, but why is heaven not in us? We say in church that the Holy Spirit came; I would hope so! We will celebrate our preachers when they say we are victorious, but where is the victory? We can celebrate the Kingdom coming, but where is it coming from? Most black folk do not like Bible study and will not attend classes; and if anything is taught for which conviction would require change, they quit! We will often go to a church because it has a big name, it is historic; so are mausoleums! We will worship those preachers who go to school to learn how to "say it," but we will not insist that they also "do it." We will say we are being loving to pastors when we allow them to be abusers, forever forgive them; and we think that this is Christian love. We will not tolerate our own people in their rage and will tell them not to be angry, which is to make them become sick as a choice; yet if someone's foot is being stepped on, we would consider it healthy for that person to scream!

These issues have to do with our roles as perpetrator, victim, and witness, as well as with our fears. Unlike the biblical Hebrews we so admire in sermon, song, and Bible study, we rarely follow the Hebrew example of openly fighting or making an exodus from those who traumatize us without end or with impunity. It is easy to see how domestic abuse is "tolerated" (kept secret) within the black church. The theological interpretation and behavioral tradition for this "toleration" is deeply rooted in the black church experience.

Perpetration and toleration

We will not address our perpetrator, victim, and witness issues in part because we think our preaching addresses everything that needs addressing. If that is our position, we can expect only so much healing. I have said that good black preaching can help set the stage for healing, but it cannot do the healing without folk also being counseled and relationshiped with, and without those things we "tolerate" being brought out into the open for all of us to deal with. Our problem here is that

Black preaching is not end-all in healing

we tend to dislike people who assist us in looking at things we are unable to look at ourselves, people who assist us in getting in touch with feelings we have been taught to deny. We are even able to reject sound doctrine if it requires challenge and growth. Those of us who are like this treat the black church as a place in which we should get our damaged needs catered to but not fulfilled!

Pastors cannot be the only healers

Not only must the day come to an end in which we think preaching is the end-all, but also in which we think only pastors can be our spiritual healers. First of all, the pastors cannot do it all alone; they themselves often fall victim to the character and demand of congregations and to the silliness of members who need and enjoy soap-opera confusion and commercial entertainment. In such an environment, the sincere and healthy pastor can be discouraged. The informed pastor who understands that grieving people are particularly vulnerable, that needfulness is not to be confused with love, and that worship can cause conscious thought to relax and open a doorway to the unconscious or subconscious where healing can begin (or trauma can be re-enforced)—even that good pastor can feel helpless.

All can be soul therapists

Secondly, all of us can be soul therapists. We might not be clinically trained to do the heavy-duty, long-term therapy, such as psychoanalysis, but neither are our pastors. In any case, healthy family is for the purposes of preventing trauma and supporting the traumatized. If we believe we are God's family, that is what the church family is for: prevention and support. Family and church are the two places in the community we ought to be able to go and not get abused!

The truth is, if the church really were a healing center, people would not be leaving before they wish: because they entered the church not dressed appropriately, or looking as though they have a real problem, or are too needy, members respond by talking about them and casting them disparaging looks. When such visitors are taken in the back and asked if they want Jesus to save them and if they want to join the church, a response that they simply need to be around people who "give a damn" can get them ushered out of the church. If they refuse to leave, it can get them ignored.

Neither should members be running out of the church because they are being abused. They should be leaving only because they are healthy and are going out to help others who are not. We abuse folk even when they want to leave to help others, because we are always interested in how many we can get into church and get to stay as members, particularly tithing members. Yet who among us has seen the church that the real Jesus

Abuse in the black church

built and pastored with all his disciples sitting up in it, praying and singing hymns?

So the black church has shortcomings; we admit it. But it can be a healing center. In the beginning, black religion "acted believing" that God meant to counteract the terror of the perpetrators of chattel slavery. Under the pressures of the master-slave system, regular core-belief refills were necessary for the enslaved to prepare for and process the daily psycho-spiritual insults to their self-image. The purpose of family and culture (family being to the individual what culture is to the group) was to help the "members" learn the proven and approved patterns of core belief which guided their definition of and conduct within reality, and helped everyone acquire the material and the nonmaterial requisites of surviving and living.

Black church can be a healing center

The lesson is yet to be learned, and it is still relevant; much of the healing that remains for soul therapy to bring about in our community has to do with the mutating effects of the chattelization process. This includes its effects on our church leadership, due to the predominant theology that teaches adjustment to abuse rather than empowerment to do something about it.

Mutating effects of chattelization

Those masses among us who accept the path of coping, having opted for certainty in an uncertain world, die

Mere coping

to challenges and risks associated with a life open to spiritual potential. Safety and security are foremost for them, even if it means living in the isolation of an unfulfilled life or living in denial about injustice. What results from the spreading of this survivalism, is that there are fewer people who can get things done, fewer who can be trusted for guidance, fewer who can motivate others, and fewer who have the skills a community direly needs. In reality, there are few leaders. But, of course, there are many gatekeepers! There are a few who are capable of motivating, yet there are many more who will not even let them!

Why are there so few? Because coping, if it goes on too long, often turns into co-dependency, which means depending on someone or something that is undependable: people, cultures, institutions, and systems that provide and protect on the condition that they are served without challenge to unjust policies and actions. A tradition of co-dependent core belief and behavior can become the standard as it is passed down through generations.

Our real difficulty lies in overcoming the intergenerational effects of the chattelization process. And this depends on our ability to understand how living in an abusive system that traumatizes us regularly can cause us to spend our entire lives in a state of re-

Overcoming intergenerational chattelization

sponding to trauma, to the degree that we get stuck there and thus help keep ourselves chattel by breaking any internal efforts at healing or liberation.

We must also understand that while white Christians were busy claiming that the dark heathen was possessed by sin and sickness, the sin and sickness of racism had infected the very bowels of white Christianity in America. Black folks were forced to internalize some acceptable combination of the soul-diminishing effects of this sin and sickness; our having done so has resulted in a wide variety of trauma-related psychological disorders occurring among us which are now deemed normative by many: rage, confusion, and self-defeating violence. In the meantime, while our role in this master-slave system has been to internalize our own degradation, the role of whites has been to legitimize, sanitize, and institutionalize their resultant advantages.

This latter role was intended to alleviate guilt for the generations to come, but it did not free co-dependent white America from the unhealthy effects of having to accept institutional force and violence as reasonable tools of societal control. And it especially did not free co-dependent white America from having to accept the possibility of violence coming home to roost. The possibility of rebounding violence has left whites feeling vul-

Oppression coming home to roost

nerable and angry, and thus has rendered them victim to such social diseases as family abuse, alcoholism, and suicide. What makes matters worse for them is that blacks are still achieving within the system, despite the systemic roadblocks; a fact which says to whites that there exists an even greater threat of what we might do once our shackles are completely shaken off, and perhaps the roles are reversed.

This fear is very real among whites who shudder at the thought of losing their advantage and privilege, but it is all the more real for those whites in the lower socioeconomic echelons who do not readily experience their advantage and privilege. All of them share one similarity, however, whether or not they experience their advantage and privilege: while claiming love as their most central religious principle, they will hate black people without remorse or repentance, and divide and conquer black people; they will hunt down black people, burn black people at the stake, blow up black people in churches, and castrate black people in various forms of public and private (and now high-tech) inquisitions.

White fear

What we must use to neutralize and remove life's dissonance of this sort and to generate the healing process we so very much need, are the spiritual antiseptics within our core beliefs, antiseptics that are capable of handling those life-threatening infections caused by the processes of internalized victimization. In this regard, the black church leadership and followership must seriously reinvest in putting the "soul" back into the best and most healthy of our core beliefs, of which sometimes only a shell of rhetoric remains. This will allow necessary resources to be available in our personal/family bio-psycho-socio-spiritual health packages for the cultivation of wellness and prosperity among us even while our humanity remains under attack.

Putting the "soul" back into the best and most healthy of our core beliefs will require that the black church be a location where life is consistent and dependable, needs are answered, improvement is rewarded, autonomy is permissible, anger is healthy, and fear is under control. Unresolved conflict, which especially plagues us with the dis-ease of grief, encourages a fear-centered life, in which we are steadily on the lookout for things that reflect or represent what is feared. In extreme cases, our fears are fused into every aspect of our personalities and can become so overwhelming that pointing the finger at others, imitating behavior that is the source of our fears, separating feeling from fact, and physical illness can become life-standards for us. Although I do believe that the only place the Devil can get us is where we are afraid and

Putting back the soul

Requirements for a soulful black church

CONCLUSION

cannot admit it, we have good reason to be fearful; yet our families and communities have the potential, through the practice of soul therapy, to help us resist the tendency to drift into extremes of fear by promoting safe and secure environments and viable core beliefs.

This communal aspect of soul therapy might be the reason the good Lord allows men and women to preach and the reason there were twelve disciples: people can get help in a variety of ways. The pharaoh model, in which only one "bearded" person sits on the pulpit throne, is not good for our needs in the black church. Healthy and helpful community is what we seek, for the community is best able to provide support for corrective emotional experiences and for an environment in which people will no longer feel alone in bearing their reality or remembering their trauma in order to process their hurt.

Communal aspect of soul therapy

Moreover, people nurtured by a healthy soul church and community will treasure acts of interpretation, clarification, confrontation, and advice when family or parenting deficiencies exist. Family, community, and a providential God working hand-in-hand, in and through the church, can counteract the destructive tendencies of catastrophic loss and daily insult by helping us engage in healthy response to that unacceptable bio-psycho-social injury and soul laceration called trauma.

Healing of a time-honored tradition

Healing of the kind I am describing should be understood as a time-honored tradition in African American indigenous culture, in which the health of every individual's invisible spirit is based not alone on a one-to-one relationship with God or a single man who was crucified on a cross, but on the uplifting of interpersonal relationships within the soul community. An important key in this health system is love, which should not be understood as a mere feeling, but rather as action based on certain core belief. This kind of love involves choice that is enduring because it has been enacted, while the "feeling" kind of love simply comes and goes, finding little more than words by which to express itself.

Shortcomings in ability to love

The "feeling" sort of love really ends up being a necessity, however; because our damaged self-image has obstructed our capacity for choice, our injured souls have had no freedom of choice and therefore cannot fully love. Not only can we not fully love others in our families, churches, and communities, we cannot fully love ourselves. When we cannot adequately love ourselves, we cannot give ourselves what is best for our health, even in our choice of religion. Consequently, instead of time-honored healing of a communal sort, we are too easily satisfied with individualist success-worshiping theologies administered from the pulpits and through television-ready Bible studies. Furthermore, we are too easily satisfied with middle-class Christian snobbery which produces the likes of one minister who refused a new Mercedes from a congregation because he thought a Rolls-Royce would serve him better!

As regards music and our time-honored tradition of communal healing, I have suggested that we can hear certain kinds of music and feel in our deepest parts that it sounds like "home." What is wrong with some of the music we are listening to today is the kind of "home" it reflects! If we look back over time and see whom we liked singing to us at critical stages in our historic struggle in America, we discover that much of our music portrays a "home" that is village.

Music that sounds like home

There were such times! Times when the therapy for our souls gave our masses more than mere denial, opportunism, and magic; and more than excuses for our condition, excuses being mere lies posing as truths. But everywhere around us today is evidence of our once indigenous religion being disfigured not simply by the powers of external soul assault but by the penetration or internalization of unchecked assault, which is our own fault. The fragmentation and loss of the indigenous foundation of African American culture, that we have permitted, insures community impotence and frigidity in matters of justice, that highest of pragmatical community values. Healing the community is at the heart of attempts at justice.

Healing an attempt at justice

Our church memberships understand theoretically what we are entrusted to do as regards justice: bring the "good news" to those who are poor in any and every area of their humanity, heal the broken-souled, make known to the spiritual captives how they can be released in body and mind, and to those who have eyes but cannot see how they can regain their vision. Proactively, we are to comfort and console all who mourn, respond to the psychological power of others to define and limit our individual and collective dreams, be for our people a source of joy and beauty instead of sorrow and shame. As trees of right relationships, specific plantings of God, we must help the downtrodden among us to rebuild our ruins, raise up our desolations, and repair our generations felled by grief.

Call of the soul therapist

~ *Postscript* ~

Have you ever noticed the smile that struggles to be free in the corners of the mouth of someone who has abused you? Justice to such a person means winning all the time. The hidden smile tells you that he or she enjoys your pain and suffering. The laugh, if it ever finds full expression, tells you this person feels secure in the action of injustice. Unrepentant perpetrators are not people of good character.

Unrepentant perpetrators have bad character

From a position of power and advantage, perpetrators remind those holding third-class tickets that no rescue boats are available for them on the luxury liner. So grand is their Titanic and their position in life that they feel justified in their sense of superiority to all less well-bred travelers. In a crisis, their own survival cancels the idealistic rhetoric they have often used at the captain's table.

The degree to which such perpetrators will go to get and keep privilege is so frightening that most of the servant class will, like the disciples of Jesus, deny they know the truth. Ironically, it is the servant class that fights the hardest to make sure the master class survives when the ship strikes an iceberg and begins to sink.

The brave and the honorable, people of good character, go down with the ship, if that is what is necessary for others to be saved. The unwanted, untouchable, and ugly, if not locked below deck, will freeze to death in the iceberg-filled sea. Life jackets only prolong the inevitable for those without means or hope.

In times like these, the hopeful imagine themselves as the ones who will be rescued, and they hold on against all odds in the midst of the wasted humanity. And lo, one lone rescue boat, captained by a well-positioned caring soul, returns to the scene just in case any among the frozen have survived.

The person who abuses us, who likes the way such abuse makes him or her feel and who needs others to be in a constant state of grief, will not return to offer help. Only the person of good character, the kind soul who insures the life of hope, will do so.

What did you experience when the Titanic went down? Do you know that the Titanic is always sinking for those stuck in their grief? In the face of such adversity, are you a person of good character?

Soul therapists have good character

Good character is a sign of a healthy self-image, which is rooted in proved and approved core belief. The following twelve elements are signs of a healthy character in people ready to achieve their full human potential as purveyors of justice in the titanic world and as soul therapists.

Deep roots in search of freedom

1) Deep Roots in Search of Freedom. The tree of life must grow deep roots of its own. The roots must be

anchored well enough that they are dependable. Freedom is more than a release from limitation; it is the proactive replacement of external restraints with inner self-control. It means taking charge of co-creating the highest form of ourselves. Powerlessness and mediocrity are signs of inadequate resources. Deep roots and life-supporting limbs in search of freedom require adequate spiritual reserves.

2) God-Centered Self-Esteem and Other-Appreciation. To be a child of God is to be sacred. Healthy self-esteem will not allow plagues and pestilence—which can be mental, physical, or spiritual (symbolic or real)—to enter into sacred areas. Thinking too much of ourselves to hide the fact that we do not think enough of ourselves is a sign that plagues and pestilence have entered our sacred areas. Each of us must decide whether life will be a consecration or desecration in our care.

God-centered self-esteem

3) Ability to See the Invisible. Until we can see and appreciate both the prose and the poetry present in living, we will be limited in potential. The ability to see honestly and clearly all around the inside and outside of ourselves opens the way to seeing the impossible possible that makes the invisible visible. The nature of our response to challenge and temptation is a sign of our inner character.

Ability to see the invisible

Respect for privilege of living

4) Respect for the Privilege of Living. A respect for the privilege of living is evident when a radiant goodness is apparent. The teacher who considers teaching a privilege, the student who considers learning a privilege, and the friend who considers friendship a privilege will usually radiate goodness. Happiness is a by-product of radiant goodness and the release of our latent potential and powers.

Commitment to self-improvement

5) Commitment to Self-Improvement and Purposeful Living. People of character grapple with growth and purpose for their lives. They learn to trust themselves and not circumstances. They understand the difference between possession and ownership, possession being material and ownership being psychological and spiritual. Commitment to self-improvement and purposeful living is usually present when we live with the full understanding that the soul is our whole invisible personality which thinks, purposes, loves, and searches life's heights and depths.

Quest for discipline

6) Quest for Discipline. Recovery from a lack of discipline is a terrific process. Lack of discipline has a binding power because of the less-than-good habits it spawns and because it perverts the ability to see straight. Lack of discipline is contagious, and it hardens and eventually becomes callous. If left unchecked, lack of disci-

pline turns us into walking dead. Discipline is present when goals are being met and reset in a positive way again and again.

7) Always Seeking the Greatest Good. Above-average living is often the narrow road less traveled. It means resisting the temptation to reduce ourselves to the lowest common denominator: living without a well-defined vision, seeking the average, and focusing on the worst scenario. Seeking the greatest good means overcoming the preservation of our own lives and the tendency merely to follow the crowd.

Always seeking the greatest good

8) Refusing to Construct Life Out of the Negative and Passive. This requires transforming primitive instincts into positives instead of negatives. The sexual instinct can be channeled into artistic and social creativeness. Fear can be elevated into respect for equals and elders. Selfishness can be enlarged to include all of creation and not just our individual selves.

Refusing to construct life out of the negative

9) Quest for Magnanimity. This requires overcoming super-sensitivity to hurt and conquering morbid fascination with slights, hurts, insults, and revenge (or finding happiness only in thoughts of getting even). It means that we behave with the realization that vindictiveness makes us the slaves of our enemies. Instead, we quest to rise above all of this to the realm of our better qualities.

Quest for magnanimity

Owning the past

10) Owning the Past. This means living fully in the present with an eye on the future and a student's attitude of inquiry toward our past. We need to resist glorifying or romanticizing the past, yet we must also be able to distinguish between our blood heredity and our social inheritance.

Choice to see things through

11) The Choice to See Things through to Their Best Conclusion. This requires an appreciation for the winds of life. The taller trees wrestle with storms and tempests just as much, if not more than, the short shielded mustard bush. This characteristic is present when patience and perseverance are second nature to us when we are faced with a challenge or problem.

Twelfth test

12) The Twelfth Test Is To Be Discovered.

Thank you.

~ *Bibliography* ~

Achterberg, Jeanne. *Imagery in Healing: Shamanism and Modern Medicine*. Boston: Shambhala, 1985.

Akbar, Na'im. *Chains and Images of Psychological Slavery*. Jersey City: New Mind Productions, 1991.

Allen, Theodore W. *The Invention of the White Race: Racial Oppression and Social Control, Volume I*. New York: Verso, 1994.

Allport, Gordon. *The Nature of Prejudice*. New York: Addison-Wesley, 1988.

Asante, Molefi Kete. *African American History: A Journey of Liberation*. Maywood: Peoples Publishing Group, 1995.

Baltzell, E. Digby. *The Protestant Establishment: Aristocracy & Caste in America*. New York: Random House, 1964.

Blassingame, John W. *The Slave Community: Plantation Life in the Antebellum South*. New York: Oxford University Press, 1972.

_____, ed. *Slave Testimony: Two Centuries of Letters, Speeches, Interviews, and Autobiographies*. Baton Rouge: Louisiana State University, 1977.

Branden, Nathaniel. *The Six Pillars of Self-Esteem*. New York: Bantam, 1994.

Brener, Anne. *Mourning and Mitzvah: A Guided Journal for walking the Mourner's Path through Grief to Healing*. Woodstock: Jewish Lights Publishing, 1993.

Brodzinsky, David M., Marshall D. Schechter, and Robin Marantz Henig. *Being Adopted: The Lifelong Search for Self.* New York: Doubleday/Anchor, 1992.

Brown, Joanne Carlson, and Carole R. Bohn, eds. *Christianity, Patriarchy, and Abuse: A Feminist Critique.* Cleveland: Pilgrim Press, 1989.

Cameron, Norman. *Personality Development and Psychopathology: A Dynamic Approach.* Boston: Houghton Mifflin, 1963.

Cannon, Katie G. *Black Womanist Ethics.* Atlanta: Scholars Press, 1988.

Carlson, Benjamin Shield, ed. *Healers on Healing.* Los Angeles: Jeremy P. Tarcher, 1989.

Chopra, Deepak. *Quantum Healing: Exploring the Frontiers of Mind/Body Medicine.* New York: Bantam Books, 1989.

Cooper-Lewter, Nicholas, and Henry H. Mitchell. *Soul Theology: The Heart of American Black Culture.* San Francisco: Harper and Row, 1986. Re-published Abingdon Press, 1991.

Copher, Charles B. *Black Biblical Studies.* Chicago: Black Light Fellowship, 1993.

Cramer, Raymond. *The Psychology of Jesus and Mental Health.* Grand Rapids: Pyranee Books, 1959.

Davis, David Brion. *The Problem of Slavery in the Age of Revolution, 1770-1823.* Ithaca: Cornell University Press, 1975.

Deloria, Jr., Vine. *God is Red: A Native View of Religion.* Golden: Fulcrum Publishing, 1994.

DeYoung, Curtiss Paul. *Coming Together: The Bible's Message in an Age of Diversity*. Valley Forge: Judson Press, 1995.

Diop, Cheikh Anta. *Civilization or Barbarism: An Authentic Anthology*. New York: Lawrence Hill Books, 1991.

Dossey, Larry. *Meaning & Medicine: Lessons from a Doctor's Tales of Breakthrough and Healing*. New York: Bantam Books, 1991.

Dutton, Donald G, with Susan K. Golant. *The Batterer: A Psychological Profile*. New York: Basic Books, 1995.

McGaa, Eagle Man, ed. *Mother Earth Spirituality: Native American Paths to Healing Ourselves and Our World*. San Francisco: Harper, 1990.

Erikson, Erik. *The Life Cycle Completed: A Review*. New York: Norton, 1985.

Everstine, Diana Sullivan, and Louis Everstine. *Sexual Trauma in Children and Adolescents: Dynamics and Treatment*. New York: Brunner/Mazel Publishers, 1989.

_____. *The Trauma Response: Treatment of Emotional Injury*. New York: Norton, 1993.

Felder, Cain Hope, ed. *Stony the Road We Trod: African American Biblical Interpretation*. Minneapolis: Fortress, 1991.

Forward, Susan, Craig Buck. *Toxic Parents: Overcoming Their Hurtful Legacy and Reclaiming Your Life*. New York: Bantam Books, 1989.

Fosdick, Harry Emerson. *Twelve Tests of Character*. New York: Richard R. Smith, 1931.

Franklin, John Hope. *The Color Line: Legacy for the Twenty-First Century.* Columbia: University of Missouri Press, 1993.

Fredrickson, George M. *The Black Image in the White Mind: The Debate on Afro-American Character and Destiny, 1817-1914.* Hanover: Wesleyan University Press, 1971.

Fulop, Timothy E., and Albert J. Raboteau, eds. *African-American Religion: Interpretive Essays in History and Culture.* New York: Routledge, 1997.

Goleman, Daniel. *Emotional Intelligence: Why It Can Matter More Than IQ.* New York: Bantam, 1995.

Grant, Jacquelyn. *White Women's Christ and Black Women's Jesus: Feminist Christology and Womanist Response.* Atlanta: Scholars Press, 1989.

Greene, Robert, and Joost Elffers. *The 48 Laws of Power.* New York: Viking, 1998.

Gregoire, Henri. *On the Cultural Achievements of Negroes.* Trans. Thomas Cassirer and Jean-Francois Briere. Amherst: University of Massachusetts Press, 1996.

Grier, William H., and Price M. Cobbs, *Black Rage.* New York: Basic Books, 1968.

Gurman, Alan S., and David P. Kniskern, eds. *Handbook of Family Therapy, Volume 2.* New York: Brunner/Mazel Publishers, 1991.

Hacker, Andrew. *Two Nations, Black and White, Separate, Hostile, Unequal.* New York: Charles Scribner's Sons, 1992.

Hawkins, Del I., Roger J. Best, and Kenneth A. Coney. *Consumer Behavior: Implications for Marketing Strategy.* Homewood: Richard D. Irwin, 1989.

Hood, Robert E. *Begrimed and Black: Christian Traditions on Blacks and Blackness.* Minneapolis: Fortress, 1994.

Hopkins, Dwight N., and George Cummings. *Cut Loose Your Stammering Tongue: Black Theology in the Slave Narratives.* Maryknoll: Orbis Books, 1991.

Jacobs, Louis. *The Jewish Religion: A Companion.* Oxford: Oxford University Press, 1995.

Jampolsky, Lee. *Healing the Addictive Mind.* Berkeley: Celestial Arts, 1991.

Jantz, Gregory L. *Healing the Scars of Emotional Abuse.* Grand Rapids: Revell, 1995.

Johnson, David, and Jeff VanVonderen. *The Subtle Power of Spiritual Abuse.* Minneapolis: Bethany House Publishers, 1991.

Jordan, Winthrop D. *White Over Black: American Attitudes Toward the Negro, 1550-1812.* Chapel Hill: University of North Carolina Press, 1968.

————. *The White Man's Burden: Historical Origins of Racism in the United States.* New York: Oxford University Press, 1974.

Kakar, Sudhir. *The Inner World: A Psycho-Analytic Study of Childhood and Society in India.* Delhi: Oxford University Press, 1981.

Kaslow, Florence W., ed. *Handbook of Relational Diagnosis and Dysfunctional Family Patterns*. New York: John Wiley, 1996.

Kennedy, Stetson. *Jim Crow Guide: The Way It Was*. Boca Raton: Florida Atlantic Press, 1990.

King, Wilma. *Stolen Childhood: Slave Youth in Nineteenth-Century America*. Bloomington: Indiana University Press, 1996.

Konopka, Gisela. *Social Group Work: A Helping Process*. Englewood Cliffs: Prentice-Hall, 1972.

Kreisman, Jerold J., and Hal Straus. *I Hate You - Don't Leave Me: Understanding the Borderline Personality*. Los Angeles: The Body Press, 1989.

Kroger, William S. *Clinical and Experimental Hypnosis: In Medicine, Dentistry and Psychology*. Philadelphia: J. B. Lippincott, 1963.

Lasch, Christopher. *The Culture of Narcissism: American Life in an Age of Diminishing Expectations*. New York: Norton, 1980.

Lerner, Michael. *Surplus Powerlessness*. Oakland: Institute for Labor & Mental Health, 1986.

Lincoln, C. Eric. *Race, Religion, and the Continuing American Dilemma*. New York: Hill and Wang, 1984.

Lincoln, C. Eric, and Lawrence H. Mamiya. *The Black Church in the African American Experience*. Durham: Duke University Press, 1990.

Linn, Edmund Holt. *Preaching as Counseling, The Unique Method of Harry Emerson Fosdick*. Valley Forge: Judson Press, 1966.

Lockard, Joan S., and Delroy L. Paulhus, eds. *Self-Deception: An Adaptive Mechanism?* Englewood Cliffs: Prentice Hall, 1988.

Majors, Richard, and Janet Mancini Billson. *Cool Pose: The Dilemmas of Black Manhood in America.* New York: Lexington Books, 1992.

Maslow, Abraham H. *Religions, Values, and Peak-Experiences.* New York: Penguin Books, 1976.

Mazrui, Ali A. *The Africans: A Triple Heritage.* London: BBC Publications, 1986.

McCann, I. Lisa, and Laurie Anne Pearlman. *Psychological Trauma and the Adult Survivor: Theory, Therapy, and Transformation.* New York: Brunner/Mazel Publishers, 1990.

McGuire, Meredith B. *Religion: The Social Context, Third Edition.* Belmont: Wadsworth Publishing Company, 1992.

McKenzie, J. G. *Nervous Disorders and Religion.* London: George Allen and Unwin, 1951.

McKitrick, Eric L., ed. *Slavery Defended: The Views of the Old South.* Englewood Cliffs: Prentice-Hall, Inc., 1963.

McManus, Edgar J. *Black Bondage in the North.* Syracuse: Syracuse University Press, 1973.

Miller, Dusty. *Women Who Hurt Themselves: A Book of Hope and Understanding.* New York: Basic Books, 1994.

Missildine, W. Hugh. *Your Inner Child of the Past.* New York: Simon and Schuster, 1963.

Nelson, C. Ellis. *How Faith Matures.* Louisville: Westminster/John Knox Press, 1989.

Noll, Joyce Elaine. *Company of Prophets: African American Psychics, Healers and Visionaries.* St. Paul: Llewellyn Publications, 1991.

Oates, Wayne E. *The Psychology of Religion.* Waco: Word Books, 1973.

Our Feet Walk the Sky: Women of the South Asian Diaspora. San Francisco: Aunt Lute Books, 1993.

Pagels, Elaine. *The Origin of Satan.* New York: Random House, 1995.

Paley, Vivian Gussin, Wade Clark Roof, Jane P. Ward, and Gerard A. Pottebaum, *Exploring the Spirituality of Childhood.* Loveland: Spiritual Life of Children Institute, 1998.

Panati, Charles. *Sacred Origins of Profound Things: The Stories Behind the Rites and Rituals of the World's Religions.* New York: Penguin Group, 1996.

Peck, M. Scott. *People of The Lie: The Hope for Healing Human Evil.* New York: Simon and Schuster, 1983.

Pelletier, Kenneth R. *Sound Mind, Sound Body: A New Model for Lifelong Health.* New York: Simon and Schuster, 1994.

Perkins, Useni Eugene. *Harvesting New Generations: The Positive Development of Black Youth.* Chicago: Third World Press, 1985.

Pfister, Oscar. *Christianity and Fear: A Study in History and in the Psychology and Hygiene of Religion.* London: George Allen and Unwin, 1948.

Pieterse, Jan Nederveen. *White on Black: Images of Africa and Blacks in Western Popular Culture.* New Haven: Yale University Press, 1992.

Pinderhughes, Elaine. *Understanding Race, Ethnicity, and Power: The Key to Efficacy in Clinical Practice.* New York: The Free Press, 1989.

Pinkerton, Judith. *The Sound of Healing.* Brooklyn: Alliance Publishing, 1996.

Poling, James Newton. *The Abuse of Power: A Theological Problem.* Nashville: Abingdon Press, 1993.

Pollard, Alton B. III. *Mysticism and Social Change.* New York: Peter Lang, 1992.

Powell, Thomas. *The Persistence of Racism in America.* Lanham: Rowan and Littlefield, 1993.

Prinzing, Fred, and Anita Prinzing. *Mixed Messages: Responding to Interracial Marriage.* Chicago: Moody Press, 1991.

Roediger, David R., ed. *Black on White: Black Writers on What It Means to Be White.* New York: Schocken, 1998.

Rossi, Ernest L., ed. *Milton H. Erickson: The Collected Papers of Milton H. Erickson on Hypnosis, Volume 4.* New York: Irvington Publishers, 1989.

Rossi, Ernest Lawrence. *The Psychobiology of Mind-Body Healing.* New York: Norton, 1993.

Russell, Kathy, Midge Wilson, and Ronald Hall. *The Color Complex: The Politics of Skin Color Among African Americans.* New York: Harcourt Brace Jovanovich, 1992.

Schaef, Anne Wilson, and Diane Fassel. *The Addictive Organization*. New York: Harper and Row, 1990.

Sinkler, George. *The Racial Attitudes of American Presidents: From Abraham Lincoln to Theodore Roosevelt.* Garden City: Anchor, 1972.

Sjoo, Monica, and Barbara Mor. *The Great Cosmic Mother: Rediscovering the Religion of the Earth.* San Francisco: Harper, 1987.

Spencer, Jon Michael. *Protest and Praise: Sacred Music of Black Religion.* Minneapolis: Fortress Press, 1990.

_____. *Re-Searching Black Music.* Knoxville: University of Tennessee Press, 1997.

Staudacher, Carol. *Beyond Grief: A Guide for Recovering from the Death of a Loved One.* Oakland: New Harbinger Publications, 1987.

Tatum, Beverly Daniel. *Why Are All the Black Kids Sitting Together in the Cafeteria?* New York: Basic Books, 1997.

Taylor, J. Troup. *The Prophetic Families, or, The Negro: His Origin, Destiny and Status.* Atlanta: The Foote and Davis Printing Company, 1895.

Thorpe, Earle E. *Slave Religion, Spirituals, and C. G. Jung.* Durham: Harrington Publications, 1983.

Thurman, Howard. *Jesus and The Disinherited.* Richmond, Ind.: Friends United Press, 1981.

Tillich, Paul. *The Courage To Be.* New Haven: Yale University Press, 1952.

Tise, Larry E. *Proslavery: A History of the Defense of Slavery in America, 1701-1840.* Athens: University of Georgia Press, 1987.

Van Sertima, Ivan, ed. *Blacks in Science: Ancient and Modern.* New Brunswick: Transaction Books, 1990.

Wade, Richard C. *Slavery in the Cities: The South 1820-1860.* New York: Oxford University Press, 1964.

Walker, Barbara G. *The Woman's Dictionary of Symbols and Sacred Objects.* San Francisco: Harper, 1988.

Weatherhead, Leslie D. *The Transforming Friendship: A Book about Jesus and Ourselves.* Nashville: Abingdon Press, 1990.

White, Shane. *Somewhat More Independent: The End of Slavery in New York City, 1770-1810.* Athens: University of Geogia Press, 1991.

Williams, James G. *The Bible, Violence, and the Sacred: Liberation from the Myth of Sanctioned Violence.* Valley Forge: Trinity Press International, 1991.

Worden, J. William. *Grief Counseling and Grief Therapy.* New York: Springer Publishing Company, 1991.

Yalom, Irvin D. *The Theory and Practice of Group Psychotherapy.* New York: Basic Books, 1985.

~ *Index* ~

American Dream, 87-89

Andersen, Hans Christian, 1

anger, 17, 27, 43

black church: creation of village in, 46, 128; entertainment in, 70, 71; grief in, 8-9, 29-30, 69; healing forms of, 97, 111-13, 116, 117, 119, 120, 125; limited definition of, 72, 118, 119-20; shortcomings of, 74-75, 98, 116-18, 120. *See also* spiritual abuse

black community, 8, 45, 69, 76, 83, 125, 127-28. *See also* village

black identity, 22. *See also* indigenousness

black male-female relationships, 32

class issues, 23, 71, 72, 127

consumerism, 34, 58-59

coping, 21, 92, 121; masks, 3, 40-41; mechanisms, 13, 14, 96-97, 116; styles, 5

core beliefs, 28, 36, 44, 45-46, 47, 91, 121, 123-24, 126; and good character, 13-34; intergenerational, 51-52, 104, 114; reaffirmed in music, 109

dancing, 41, 104

entertainment, 13, 57; and spiritual abuse, 62-64; and worship, 70

INDEX

fear, 28-29, 35-36, 122-23, 124-25

grief: causes of, 6-8, 17; generational, 44; resolution of, 36

grief work: interference in, 24, 38-39, 41-45, 57-58, 68, 124; stages of, 19-20

indigenousness, 22, 41, 45-46, 67, 68, 82, 92-93, 96, 103; and community, 84-85, 126; and place, 69, 72, 127; thwarting of, 47, 48-49. *See also* village

intrauterine experiences, 79-80, 81

Jesus, as white, 63, 84

Jews, 72, 117; grieving culture of, 68-69

Judaism, 72, 84

King, Martin Luther, Jr., 87-77

love, pretense of, 38, 64-65, 90, 106, 116-17, 123

March on Washington, 87

master-slave relationship, 10, 21, 22, 26-27, 28, 33, 44, 73; co-dependency, 55-59, 88, 93-95; narcissism in 59-61. *See also* sponsor-trustee relationship

music, 12, 41, 70, 103-04; ministry of, 104-05. *See also* soul therapy

passive-aggressive strategies, 31-32

pastors: abuses of, 65-66, 98; adoration of, 9-10; as spiritual healers, 118; as trustees, 22

perpetrator-victim-witness relationship, 21, 28-31, 64, 98-102, 129; intergenerational, 98-100 prophetic religion, 70-71

provider-protector relationship, 25-27, 30, 117

renaming, 48-49

rites of passage, 111, 113-14; black church as, 111-13

Roots, 49

Rosewood, 80-86, 91, 96

self-esteem, 36-37, 63-64, 76, 82-83, 131

self-hate, 30-31, 66-67

sexism, 11, 125

soul, 77, 82, 124

soul therapy: origins of, 109-111; and music, 104-111, 127

spiritual: growth, 112-13; healing, 75-78, 113; versus religious, 49-50

spiritual abuse, 77; defined, 50; in the black church, 11, 38

spirituality, 45-46; defined, 49-50; desired form of, 73-74

sponsor-trustee relationship, 22-24, 27, 33, 44, 73; co-dependency, 55-59, 96. *See also* master-slave relationship

survival strategies, 33-34, 121

Tarzan, 63, 66

televangelism, 15, 126-27

Temptations, 107-08

terrorism, 48-49, 80-81, 84, 86

trauma, 14, 18, 19, 67, 82, 115-16, 122, 125; counteracting, 119, 125; domino, 82; post response, 65, 115

ugliness personified, 1-5, 33, 45, 47, 49, 129-30

victimization, 42; internalized, 23-24, 32, 67, 83, 86-87, 124. *See also* self-hate

village, 45-46, 69, 127. *See also* black community

waiting to exhale, 43

white church racism, 53, 60-61, 65, 100-01, 122

white racism, 86, 122-23; violence of, 122

womb, 17-18, 34-35, 79-80

word-images, 32-33, 34-35